MW00396939

BEING A DISTANCE GRANDPARENT
A Book for ALL Generations

Helen Ellis M.A.

First published in Great Britain by Summertime Publishing

© Helen Ellis, 2021

All rights reserved. No part of this publication may be reproduced, stored in or introduced into a retrieval system or transmitted, in any form, or by any means (electronic, mechanical, photocopying, recording or otherwise) without the prior written permission from the publisher.

This book is sold subject to the condition that it shall not, by way of trade or otherwise, be lent, resold, hired out or otherwise circulated without the publisher's prior consent in any form of binding or cover other than in which it is published and without a similar condition including this condition being imposed on the subsequent purchaser.

ISBN: 978-1-8381670-3-5

Cover and internal pages designed by Cath Brew at drawntoastory.com

Disclaimer

Some of the quotations from contributors have been edited for reasons of clarity. Names of some contributors have been changed for reasons of privacy.

PRAISE FOR

Being a Distance Grandparent - a Book for ALL Generations

"I loved this book and Helen's powerful message of acceptance... for a grandparenting journey that might not be what you envisioned, but is very possible, from a distance. By drawing on academic research, interviews with grandparents and her personal experience, Helen provides an in-depth and thoughtful look at what it *feels like to be grandparenting* from a distance. You will recognise yourself, your emotions and your story in this book - and when you have finished it, you are sure to feel less alone."

Kerry Byrne, Ph.D.
Founder of The Long Distance Grandparent
www.thelongdistancegrandparent.com

•••

"A masterful, fantastically well researched and well-written book on the international phenomenon of family members separated by choice or chance from participating fully in their descendant's development. With the most extensive bibliography I have seen on this topic, and instructive and valuable suggestions dealing with change, you will not be bored."

Pat Hanson, Ph.D.
Author of *Invisible Grandparenting: Leave a Legacy of Love Whether You Can Be There or Not*
www.invisiblegrandparent.com

"Distance grandparents and their families will find much to learn from in this useful and personable book. Helen Ellis clearly knows the territory and lays out a road map that points out emotional challenges, common family dynamics and practical advice, from what to have in the guest room during family visits to how to manage time zone differences."

Anne P. Copeland, Ph.D.
Founder and Director, The Interchange Institute
www.interchangeinstitute.org

• • •

"This book is a comprehensive and expansive look at what it is to live far away from your grandchildren, all the while maintaining that singular closeness we all yearn for. Ellis, a seasoned distance grandmother herself, provides great tips, perspective, and a lot of empathy for anyone who is a global or distance grandparent."

Emily Morgan
Host of The Grand Life podcast
www.thegrandlife.libsyn.com

• • •

"While globalization has brought many new opportunities for families to explore the world, it has also brought new challenges. What happens when these global journeys result in generations who used to live near one another are now separated by oceans? How do family relationships survive and thrive in this 'new normal'? This book tackles these hard questions and offers clear strategies for families to successfully navigate these previously uncharted waters."

Ruth E. Van Reken, Hon DLitt
Co-author, *Third Culture Kids, 3rd ed.*
Co-founder, Families in Global Transition, www.figt.org

"I wish I had read this book before our first translocation. This book is a well-structured, informative and knowledge-based read about distance grandparenting. Throughout the book Helen offers a broad range of perspectives as a New Zealander distance grandparent, which gives a very authentic yet disciplinary approach to the understanding of the topic. With her honesty and personal voice the book becomes a very enjoyable easy read. It is a must-read for each member of a distance family, a book you should read over and over again."

Judit Végh
Intercultural Psychology Expert

•••

"Every distance family member (and the professionals supporting them) should read this book! *Being a Distance Grandparent* fosters mutual understanding and empathy between generations through rich testimonials and precious practical tips. It is the best gift you could offer somebody separated from their family: allowing them to find a sense of belonging, and tools to create meaningful change in their relationships."

Isabelle Rampa
Clinical Psychologist working with mobile families and distance parent (mother to the 5th generation living abroad)

•••

"This book is so important to help all generations to understand each other. I really enjoyed reading it and will recommend it to all my Solo Parenting Expats."

Rhoda Bangerter
Author of *Holding the Fort Abroad*
www.amulticulturallife.com

"This is a book I wish I could have put in my parents' hands and read myself when I found out I was pregnant. We could have referenced these things over the last decade, but I didn't get to have that and neither did my family. But at least other families can now. I am looking forward to sharing this book, and future books, with distance sons, daughters, grandchildren and distance grandparents so they can focus on keeping connections across the distance."

Sundae Schneider-Bean, LLC
Intercultural Strategist and Podcaster
www.sundaebean.com

• • •

"The demography of high-income societies in the 21st century is fascinating in its implications. This book deals with an aspect that has received little attention, distance grandparenting. It provides an engaging account of the issues and helps answers the questions about "why" as well as the "how to". I thoroughly recommend this book, both for those who are already "distance grandparents" and for those who are interested."

Distinguished Professor Paul Spoonley
Massey University

• • •

"In our mobile world, more young people are growing up in communities and countries away from their grandparents and extended family. In this fascinating book, a distance grandparent discusses the hot topics related to addressing grief, building emotional resilience, supporting distance children and grandchildren, handling rituals, navigating the uncertainty of ageing and more. As a physician and parent who has raised children around the globe, this book provides thoughtful advice for those who are navigating cultures, moves and generations."

Dr. Anisha Abraham
Pediatrician and author of *Raising Global Teens: A Practical Handbook For Parenting in the 21st Century*
www.dranishaabraham.com

"This splendid book is a must-read for anyone living and working abroad, as well as those considering a long distance move or transfer to a foreign country! Helen's writing is comprehensive and lucidly organized. She has elegantly combined research, anecdotal evidence, and personal experience as a distance mother and grandmother to create a significant resource for expatriates, repatriates and third culture kids (TCKs)."

Teri Sand
Psychotherapist and founder of Transitions Therapy International
www.transitionstherapyinternational.com

•••

"This is going to be the book every international family didn't know they needed."

Keri Bloomfield
Author of *Nothing like a Dane*
www.keribloomfield.com

•••

"Even as a third-generation Distance Grandparent, through both circumstance and choice, I learnt from this book. Helen Ellis has encapsulated the issues - the complexities, the unpredictables but also the joys by helping the reader understand that ultimately *Being a Distance Grandparent* is a balancing act."

Apple Gidley
Author of *Expat Life Slice by Slice*
www.applegidley.com

•••

"It is amazing that Helen's book is out when we need it the most. Having raised our own children as expats the information is irreplaceable. Many of us are dealing with multi-generational distance familying without any resource books out there. This book also touches on grandparents on the move in retirement."

Julia Simens
Author of *Emotional Resilience and the Expat Child*

To my family... near and far.

CONTENTS

FOREWORD

Helen Ellis has written a timely and important book; one that is relevant to everyone.

Transnational Families - or Distance Families as Ellis calls them - are families whose members are separated by geographical distance but who strive to maintain their sense of familyhood, their emotional connection, despite that distance. Anyone who has a loved one living far away knows the heartache of longing to be together, the sense of obligation to give, but also the need to receive care and support, to 'be there' for each other, despite the distance. This is what defines family (and family-like) relationships - sharing our lives together; what leading anthropologist of kinship studies Marshall Sahlins calls "a mutuality of being". A helpful way to think about this is to ask: How can we share enough of our lives across distance that we can continue to co-narrate each other's existence? Be an integral part of a joint family history?

I grew up deeply influenced by the distance and separation at the heart of my extended Italian-Australian migrant family. My great grandmother and her three children waited 12 long years in Italy in the 1920s and 30s to be reunited with my great grandfather who migrated to Australia, and they only had letters and the occasional message from fellow migrants to keep then connected. They weren't alone in this experience; women like my great grandmother became known as the 'white widows' - their husbands were still alive, so they didn't wear black, but the absence of their menfolk made their everyday social life akin to widowhood.

I was very close to my maternal grandmother and through her I learnt about this experience of 'distance' family life. A story firmly planted in my mind is of the day she re-met her dad at the Port of Fremantle, Western Australia, aged 14 years; a man she hadn't seen since she was two years old. I was fascinated by how this family managed to stay together despite the enormous geographical distance and excruciatingly long physical absence. How did they make it work?

My own father migrated from Italy in the 1950s, leaving behind his parents and all his siblings and extended family. I grew up getting to know them through letters, postcards, and strictly timed (expensive) monthly phone calls. These routine practices of staying in touch were punctuated by cherished rituals of gift exchange at Christmas and birthdays. Then there was the long-anticipated and much-valued visit of my paternal grandmother when I was six years old, followed six years later by our first family visit to the homeland. The experience of spending time together in person was one of heightened emotions; a special time that impressed on me the significance of visits in distance family life.

Like the family of my grandparents, these distance families have always existed, but their experiences have been largely overlooked in the past. Today, there are increasing numbers - and diverse types - of families who are 'making it work' despite the challenges of distance and absence.

Ellis's book provides us with a wealth of informed and practical advice, drawing on knowledge from actual distance family experiences, including her own incisive reflections on her own experiences. There is much to learn from the families who have themselves been managing the challenges of distance and absence. These valuable insights are relevant to all of us. Once the preserve of migrants and refugees, more and more people are experiencing first-hand what it is like to be physically separated from loved ones and constrained by physical distancing, mobility lockdowns and border closures.

Ellis's book - full of heartfelt accounts and rich narratives - provides a much-needed guide to navigating these challenges for all generations. Ellis is deeply attuned to the practices and processes, opportunities and constraints, of lives lived across borders. The experiences of distance families highlight in particular the important role of media and communication technologies, and the importance of digital literacy and access, and raise compelling questions about new ways of doing and being with family. They also heighten our awareness of the impact of migration and social policy on the wellbeing of distance families, in particular the challenges of increasingly restrictive and temporary migration pathways that limit the capacity for families to be reunited.

Ellis's book is full of creativity, empathy, understanding, openness and, most importantly, ideas. It shines a light on what it means to be a distance grandparent and in so doing creates and uncovers this important social identity, holding it up for us to examine, so that we can take a close look - add it to our everyday language - see ourselves reflected in it and in so doing, better understand what it means to do and be family in today's world.

Professor Loretta Baldassar

Loretta Baldassar is Professor in the Discipline Group of Anthropology and Sociology at The University of Western Australia (UWA) and Director of the UWA Social Care and Ageing (SAGE) Living Lab. She has published extensively on transnational mobility, with a particular focus on families and caregiving across the life course. Her publications include *Transnational Families, Migration and the Circulation of Care* (with Merla, 2014); *Families Caring Across Borders* (with Baldock & Wilding, 2007); *Intimacy and Italian Migration* (with Gabaccia, 2011); and the award-winning book, *Visits Home* (MUP 2001). Baldassar is Vice President of the International Sociological Association, Migration Research Committee (31) and a Regional Editor for the leading journal *Global Networks*. Professor Baldassar was recently named one of the top 30 Australian researchers in the Social Sciences, and Research Field Leader in Human Migration (*The Australian*, 23 September 2020).

Loretta is a distance granddaughter, niece, cousin, and close friend.

A FIRST WORD: VIRAL UNCERTAINTY

The evolution of this book has been a journey of more than 20 years. I didn't just sit down one day and decide to start writing. I had a clear plan and timeline and knew what I wanted to say. By early 2020 the chapter ideas had been formulated - the nature of the content was clear and the trajectory visualised.

As I pressed the submit button on my Distance Grandparenting master's thesis in early April 2020, and tidied my office shelves in readiness to start this book, the world of Distance Grandparenting was flipping on its head. In fact the world was changing... likely forever.

My carefully-crafted plans were rattled like the sinister rumble of an earthquake. World history was transitioning from what we had always known to a ruinous, rudderless limbo. The nature of the Distance Grandparenting world I planned to write about had twisted on its axis.

The COVID-19 pandemic has affected the craft of every researcher, writer, scholar, film-maker, television producer - anyone telling stories of people. I was not alone. Each and every one has asked themself: *What do I do with the pandemic?*

In *Tread Softly For You Tread On My Life,* late New Zealand historian Michael King (1945-2004) considered questions that trouble discerning writers and readers, such as: "What does one owe to one's subjects and to one's readers?" He cited American social historian and writer John Dos Passos and provided me with the answer to my pandemic dilemma: "In times of change when there is a quicksand of fear under people's reasoning, a sense of continuity with generations gone before can stretch like a lifeline across an alarming present." What Dos Passos is saying is that it's necessary to look back, so as to be able to look forward.

That's what I've decided to do with the COVID-19 pandemic. So little has previously been documented about Distance Grandparenting, that before I observe the present, or make predictions about the future, it's necessary to address what *is* and *has been*. Whatever is new or altered in the future will be judged and compared to... by what *was*.

I will revisit the pandemic at the close of this book.

ABOUT THIS BOOK

This is a book about how it is *being* a Distance Grandparent. It is written by a Distance Grandparent and published by a Distance Parent and Distance Child. Research findings and anecdotal evidence feature, along with a little easy-read academic research, to give the book a smattering of scholarly foundation. I ask global Distance Grandparents: "How is Distance Grandparenting for you?"

This broad question can be answered in a myriad of ways, and that's exactly what happened. Topics include communication, loss, grief, acceptance, absence, presence and co-presence. I explore the senses, envy and emotional resilience. Relationships are put under the microscope and viewed from all angles. *Being there* is paramount to Distance Grandparents: supporting their children through good times and crises. Rituals, traditions and the meaning of things are all addressed. The to-ing and fro-ing of travel is well documented along with ponderings of money and the uncertainty of ageing. I finish by answering some of what I call the 'Big-Picture Questions' and give you a peek into the lives of your distance children and grandchildren. No stone is left unturned.

As a Distance Grandparent you've already discovered that challenges crop up for which there is no magical solution. Here and there, advice will be given. Please use my advice as one option. Only you know your distance family and what is best for everyone. What I *can* tell you is once you have made peace with your Distance Grandparenting package, creative solutions to whatever comes along won't be so hard to find.

This book has been written for *all* generations. If you are reading this and you are a 'middle generation' (distance son or distance daughter living away from home) or a distance grandchild, I encourage you to read further and own a copy. I have come to appreciate there's guilt about leaving one's family behind - it's never far from the minds of most migrants and expats. What better way to reduce this unfortunate burden than by gaining a deeper understanding of your parents' lot? Knowledge and empathy, combined, is an all-powerful force.

I want this book to be a friend: one of those books you'll likely pick up again as your distance family dynamics shift, age and mature. If you have friends who are Distance Grandparents, I urge you to say, "You need to acquire your own copy."

Grandparents are of course not the only significant relatives for distance families. Siblings, great grandparents, aunts, uncles, godparents and cousins are all important. The book's narrative specifically addresses the concerns and realities of Distance Parents and Distance Grandparents but the principles could just as easily apply to other extended family. All connections matter. Please adapt this book in a way that works for you.

For a tidy read you may start at the beginning; however, if you are initially attracted to a topic further on, go for it. You won't get lost.

Storytelling

Professor Carolyn Ellis (no relation) from the University of South Florida is a communication scholar known for her extensive research regarding autoethnography (a reflective approach to the autobiographical narrative). Her writings convinced me *my* stories had value. In other words, it's okay to talk about myself. Furthermore, Ellis explains that storytelling gives a voice to groups of people traditionally left out of social scientific inquiry. Distance Grandparents fall into this category.

Stories are intimate and personal - the way we make sense of lives, actions, history and worlds. I wanted to make sense of Distance Grandparenting... so storytelling has been a given for this project. Stories have created a-ha moments and given me direction. When I was unsure of how I should think about an intersection of thoughts, a story would appear and provide an answer.

Next to each Distance Grandparent's name you'll see a bracket noting two countries, for example (England/N.Z.). The first country, England, is where the grandparent lives. The second country, New Zealand, is where their distance family live.

Some stories are filled with sentiment and emotion; others will make you laugh and occasionally some may cause you to have a teary eye. If I have done my job right, I hope this book understands *you* when maybe there aren't many people who truly appreciate how *you* feel about your geographically-challenged family package.

Learning *how it is for others* gives reassurance to *how it is for you*.

A Disciaimer

"The idealized grandmother of today is a benign, white-haired, kindly old woman who bakes cookies; hugs little children; holds them on her lap; kisses away their "boo-boos"; knits blankets, sweaters, and booties; and never speaks an unkind word. She is helpful to her off-spring and baby-sits whenever she is needed. She is available at all times but makes herself invisible when her presence is inconvenient. She dotes on her grandchildren, hangs onto their every utterance, and is certain that they will grow up to be Einstein - or at least a doctor. She attends all of their functions and beams with pride, regardless of the quality of their performance."
Falk & Falk, *Grandparents: A New Look at the Supporting Generation*

These amusing comments (from Psychotherapist-Sociologist duo Gerhard and Ursula Adler Falk) help us paint a picture of the idealised grandmother. Their research addresses social forces and social changes of grandparenting. Although a little fanciful, their definition serves a purpose as the image of a perfect family, and how that affects expectations of what the role could, or should, be like.

At this point, I believe a disclaimer is in order. Inevitably, as the reader begins to form a picture of me as a grandmother - accompanied by the knowledge I have recently devoted a good portion of time to writing and researching grandparenthood - you might assume I am a doting 100% committed grandmother and love every aspect of this familial role. To be honest, you'd be wrong. I am by no means a disinterested grandparent but

I am nothing like the Falks' humorous definition above. I love my grandchildren, treasure being with them and savour all the memories we create - but too much of a good (or occasionally not so good) thing will, in time, have me yearning for the return of the grandchild-free parts of my world.

MY STORY

A freshness permeated the July air (winter in the Southern Hemisphere) like the senses-filled delight of unpacking new linen. The sky was a vivid blue and there wasn't a breath of wind. It was 1999 and standing in the sprawling garden of our hilltop New Zealand home on the edge of Auckland, I was ruminating. *This all feels bizarre*, I thought. I was 40 years old, the mother of two full-on teenagers and had just become a grandparent - albeit a stepgrandparent.

But there were no tiny fingers to wrap around my own. No reminder of the miracle of creation. No baby to cradle and gently breathe in its warm aura. The newborn bundle was 12,000 miles away. I was betwixt and between, in a befuddled, albeit gladdened way.

My London-based stepson, Guy, and his wife had produced their first of two offspring, a daughter called Kara. She represented the first grandchild for my husband's side of the family. We popped a bottle of French champagne at an impromptu family gathering. It was an odd sort of celebration: something, or at least someone, was missing. Our world was launching along a path some distance (excuse the pun) from the normal script. Furthermore, I most definitely had no idea it would lead to the writing of this book. Let me explain...

My husband and I are New Zealanders and this country has always been our home. My 30-plus-year-old second marriage created a blended family. We each brought to our union a son and daughter. My husband is older than me and in 1989, the year of our wedding, our children turned 21, 20, 5 and 3 years. We had no children together. Since early into our marriage, our offspring have been on the move. One or other has lived (for either months, years or permanently) in England, Scotland, Northern Ireland, Sweden, U.S.A., Thailand, Democratic Republic of Congo, Senegal, South Sudan and Pakistan.

There was little to describe as typical about our family. We were and looked an odd bunch. These days our children are in their 50s and 30s and I hope we no longer look odd - but on the other hand, we're never in the same room to be sure.

We told our children 'you can do anything' and that is exactly what they've done.

> **❝ We told our children 'you can do anything' and that is exactly what they've done. ❞**

Going back to my garden ponderings, a few months later champagne was enjoyed again when Kendra, my Edinburgh-based stepdaughter, and her Scottish husband, Colin, produced our second granddaughter, Kayley - another out of reach bundle. However, we were fortunate, as New Zealand beckoned and they moved permanently back home. A little while later our only Kiwi-born grandchild, Reyna Hannah, joined the fray.

Around the same time, the England-based family produced our first grandson, Cameron. We now had two grandchildren in New Zealand and two in England. The internet was not a part of the world and we relied on costly telephone calls, letters, faxes and photos sent in the mail, and for the next 15 years my husband and I made numerous visits to the U.K.

Many years later, my own daughter, Lucy, married an American of Northern Irish heritage and produced my first blood grandson in Bangkok. They visited New Zealand with Peter and we travelled there several times. Their second son, Gerard, arrived just after a permanent move to Atlanta, Georgia, U.S.A. We have visited the States a few times.

Just to add to the globalisation milieu, my son Robbie won a U.S. Green Card in their lottery scheme. How lucky was I? He resides in Chicago where he met his American fiancée Jennifer.

The travel gene has successfully impregnated the next generation, and more recently my Scottish-born granddaughter Kayley left New Zealand on a working holiday, retracing her steps to the city of her birth.

So, at the time of writing, three of our four children and five of our six grandchildren (aged 4 to 21) live a significant distance from New Zealand. My husband and I have quietly accepted all these comings and goings and I count 18 long-distance visits since the first one left home.

Once my daughter produced grandchildren, our roles as Distance Grandparents started to become a part of our identity. Conversations with friends frequently commenced with questions around 'how are the kids?' and 'where are you heading to next?'.

For three decades my working life focused on business ownership and the travel industry. As a high school student, my sole ambition was to gain a position in this field and I achieved my goal. Down the track I owned a niche travel company for 11 years. This delighted my accountant husband as a portion of the costs of our U.K./Europe travel to visit family could be legitimately 'written off' for business reasons. My appetite for far-flung places was fuelled through my work and has never waned. I am a planner and am never happier than working on the intricacies of a complex travel itinerary.

An Academic Odyssey

A change of direction later saw me nervously heading to university for the first time - a mature student tackling a Bachelor of Arts undergraduate degree, majoring in Social Anthropology. But first I had to learn what Anthropology was. When I understood it was about *how* and *where* people live and inhabit in relation to *who* and *what* is important to them, I knew this was my happy place. I am naturally curious about how and why families do the things they do. At an airport I am easily entertained in an Arrivals Hall matching incoming passengers with their family and friends. I eye them up and silently make a volley of assumptions, believing I have their whole package of life (as I call it) nicely evaluated.

Towards the end of the degree I was tasked to imagine a topic for a possible master's thesis. At that stage, the word *imagine* was applicable. My part-time studies had taken many years and I had absolutely no ambition for university demands to dominate my ongoing life plans. However, when my professor, also a Distance Grandparent, showed delight at my suggested topic of Distance Grandparenting, a seed was planted by her earnest comments of 'so doable' and 'you should do this'.

My initial enquiry uncovered no New Zealand research about Distance Grandparenting and little abroad. I began to see that a gap in the literature was an appealing and potentially rewarding place in which to delve. I had what academics call a heuristic interest in my research topic: a hunger to figure it out for myself. It felt that there was a story to tell and voices to be heard. Thirty-plus years ago, when our distance family journey started, my husband and I were an oddity - but now we had many acquaintances in the same situation.

The time had come to formalise my exploration of Distance Grandparenting and I nervously decided to do my master's. During 2019, overseas family visits were temporarily put on hold so I could fast-track the process. My reward at the end of it would be a catch-up trip in March 2020 to see our family in the U.S.A. Little did I know the world had other plans and that visit wouldn't happen. But that's another story for later.

Answers to the *Whys*

As I enrolled at university there remained a nagging thought: *I have an aversion to waste.* I needed to know *why* the heck I was doing my master's. Why would I tackle it as a mature student? Why would I take a year out of my life for the task? Why would I make the sacrifice of not travelling to family? Why was I spending the money on the fees and did it all have a destination? The *whys* were answered over time from a myriad of places.

Americans Katalin Szelényi and the late Robert A. Rhoads jointly researched higher education's contribution to society. They claim students have a responsibility to expand notions of global citizenship to explain *how* the increased driving force of globalisation is shaping contemporary lives. Was this me? I was a cog in this trend. Could I embrace this challenge and 'expand notions'?

Second, as an Anthropology student I had quietly followed the sometimes controversial Professor Robert Borofsky from Hawaii

Pacific University. He is famous (or should I say infamous) in Anthropology circles for coining the term 'Public Anthropology', the merging of Anthropology (academic research) and the broader public (civic engagement). Public Anthropology, he suggests, is Anthropologists striving to have a foot in both camps - so to speak. It's about doing good with what you've learnt in academia. I wanted to do good.

Later, another *why* answer arrived when I approached my research grandparents to read the final thesis draft. For ethical reasons I needed to know that they were accepting of what I had written. It was gratifying when they explained how much they gained personally from reading other Distance Grandparents' stories. The stories had given them comfort: they weren't alone with their feelings.

The conclusion to my repeated question - *Why was I doing my master's?* - was that a mainstream book needed to be written... and I would write it.

Not One Book, but Three

Separate from my interest in Distance Grandparenting I also have a curiosity about all things expat, migration and mobility. I follow blogs, listen to podcasts and read books on the subject. I began to reflect on the knowledge and insights I had gained.

My original intention was to write a single book about Distance Grandparenting. However, this broader knowledge helped me appreciate the other side of distance familying. Our distance sons and daughters, who I also refer to as the *middle generation*, have their own issues they cope with. Likewise their children, our distance grandchildren, are growing up in a world vastly different from that of our childhood. I realised if I wrote a book about Distance Grandparenting I was telling just one third of the story of distance families. Thus, a three-book, three-generational series project has evolved focusing on Distance Grandparents, distance son and daughters and distance grandchildren.

The next chapter will give Distance Parents and Distance Grandparents a wee taste into the worlds of their scattered family; a chance to increase your appreciation that there are three sides to the story.

A Postscript *Why*

A postscript *why* answer landed in my email Inbox once I gingerly started to tell the world, via social media, about my book series writing project. In June 2020, prolific expat podcaster Sundae Schneider-Bean interviewed me around the topic of Distance Grandparenting. Most of her listeners are distance sons and distance daughters. A few days after the podcast's release I emailed Sundae and thanked her for the opportunity. A comment in Sundae's response blew me away.

> *"I have listeners telling me they were 'scared' of listening - for what they would learn. A good thing they courageously listened and worked to see their parents' side of things."*
> Sundae Schneider-Bean, *Expat Happy Hour*

This was my in concrete, final *why*: why I was writing this book series. *Scared* is a powerhouse of an adjective in this context. It was then that I 100% knew this book, and the other two, needed to be written. Here was my chance, as others had said, to expand notions of global citizenship and use my academic skills to do good via Public Anthropology. Distance families would benefit by understanding how it was for the other generations. I could bring comfort to Distance Grandparents via my and others' stories so as to increase understanding and empathy between generations of distance families.

Top-Heavy Hemisphere Narratives: a Token *Down Under* Protest

When you live in the Southern Hemisphere - and the greater percentage of the world's population lives in the Northern Hemisphere - recalibrating the written and oral word around calendar seasons and certain global terminology provides constant brain gym.

When Northern Hemisphere-ites say 'we're going home for summer', Southern Hemisphere-ites automatically translate that to 'they're going home for June/July/August when it is winter for us'.

Rarely in this book will you see mention, without an explanation, of strictly Northern or Southern Hemisphere terms. As *gender neutral* is a commonly accepted contemporary term, my book series will be, as best as I can manage, *hemisphere-neutral*. Translation by either party should not be required.

THE DISTANCE FAMILY BOOK SERIES - A SNEAK PREVIEW

"Each generation develops a mindset and patterns that are unique to it."
Jim Burns, *Doing Life with Your Adult Children*

Being a Distance Grandparent - a Book for ALL Generations, as mentioned earlier, is the first of a three-book series. The other complementary titles are:

Being a Distance Son or Daughter - a Book for ALL Generations

and

Being a Distance Grandchild - a Book for ALL Generations.

Each one addresses how distance familying is for *that* generation.

The purpose of this chapter is two-fold.

- To give Distance Parents and Distance Grandparents an introduction to issues and challenges important to expats and migrants.
- To whet the appetite of Distance Parents and Distance Grandparents to increase their understanding and empathy of the worlds of their distance family.

> *"Becoming a global grandparent means that you are entering into a new life with your family. Be prepared to open up your world."*
> Peter Gosling and Anne Huscroft, *How To Be A Global Grandparent*

While Distance Grandparents are thinking, feeling, experiencing and doing everything addressed in this book, this chapter is just a wee taste of what your distance family is constantly ruminating about from afar.

Empathy

My overriding reason for writing this book series is for readers to broaden their appreciation of how life is for the *other*. By sharing our intergenerational experiences we each grow in our understanding, and more importantly empathy, for each other's worlds. This can only do good.

Researchers Huo et al. suggest in *The Journals of Gerontology* that empathy likely plays a 'promising role' strengthening close ties. Therefore, the presence of intergenerational empathy is beneficial for distance familying. They go on to say: "[...] the experiences of empathy that contain emotional components reflect a fuller and more meaningful relational experience." You'll find plenty of emotion in this book series.

> *"Empathy costs nothing, but gives a lot."*
> Bridget Romanes, Relocation Expert, New Zealand

If you are a Distance Grandparent, *this* book will help you empathise with other Distance Grandparents' experiences and feel less alone.

If you are a distance son, distance daughter or distance grandchild, *this* book will help you gain an insight into the folks back home and forever see them in a slightly different light.

For these reasons I encourage *all* generations to read *all* three books.

> **❝ I encourage *all* generations to read *all* three books. ❞**

So let's briefly look at the worlds of our distance sons, daughters and grandchildren. What follows are just some of the issues that are universal concerns to nearly all expats and migrants - your distance sons, daughters and grandchildren.

The Decision with a Capital D

The first sentence in *Expat Partner*, a career-focused mobility book by Carine Bormans and Marie Geukens, is: "What would it be like to live and work in another country?"

For most distance sons and daughters this is where it all began. A simple question, with huge ramifications. Distance sons and daughters have a choice to live in their home country or live somewhere else - and quite simply they have chosen the latter. By the time their parents learn about the potential move, the daughter or son is likely a long way down the track - past a point of no return. The move *is* going to happen.

The global lifestyle of a migrant or expat is neither easy nor glamorous. It takes resourcefulness, teamwork, determination and a lot of cultural give and take to successfully live outside of your home country.

The decision is never made lightly but once the decision *has* been made they soon learn they have to live with the consequences and possible fall-out of their choices. When a hurdle arises and things become difficult, a voice in the back of their mind reminds them, *I chose this lifestyle*. Regrettably, those inner thoughts are sometimes unhelpfully verbalised by others, including the folks back home.

In short, early acceptance by Distance Parents of the decision is beneficial for all.

Desire for Emotional Support

One theme running through virtually every expatriate/cross-cultural experience book is the desire for emotional support from those who matter to them. As humans, we tend to be tribal creatures. We prefer being surrounded by fellow members of our tribe, family or affinity group. Yet when we cannot be with our group physically, we still crave those feelings of acceptance, belonging and connection, even from afar.

"Perhaps the single strongest message we can receive, indeed the most powerful words known to mankind, are a simple, 'I love you'. As we grow up and mature into adulthood, this proclamation of love is joined by an equally powerful phrase, 'I am proud of you'. While many of us will not let the absence of these words stop us from pursuing our own particular path in life, most of us benefit greatly from hearing them."
Linda A. Janssen, *The Emotionally Resilient Expat*

In short, distance sons, daughters and grandchildren never stop craving or desiring words of encouragement and messages of love from home.

Guilt

Hands down, there isn't a mobility writer or scholar who does not profess the strongest emotion global citizens experience is guilt - guilt about the left behind family. This is a dynamic I would suggest is seldom thought about by the folks back home.

As explained by Linda Janssen in *The Emotionally Resilient Expat*, "When our loved ones are hurting, guilt exposes itself as one of the strongest and most corrosive of human emotions." Just as *Change is a Constant Companion* for Distance Grandparents, *Guilt is a Constant Companion* for distance sons and daughters. It will form a chapter in my *Being a Distance Son or Daughter - a Book for ALL Generations*.

"My choice to live overseas means I missed my grandpa's funeral. I missed two cousins' weddings. I wasn't there when each of my parents went through cancer diagnoses, treatments, and all-clears. I have cousins I've never met [...] And then comes the guilt. Knowing that I can only blame myself. That I'm the one who decided to go. That I could be closer but chose not to be. Knowing I valued something more highly than being near the family members I love so dearly. That's a hard truth to face - and yet also a hard one to escape!"
Tanya Crossman, *Misunderstood*

In short, guilt is *big*.

The Mediating Anxious Feelings Pie

In the next chapter I talk of *The Distance Family Thinking Pie*. This is an imaginary pie, sliced in three - the size of each slice represents how much each generation (grandparents, parents and grandchildren) spend time and energy *thinking* about each other. Distance Grandparents generally earn the biggest slice and do the most thinking.

It could be assumed, therefore, Distance Grandparents also consume the biggest slice of an imaginary *Mediating Anxious Feelings Pie*. Surprisingly, the grandparents take a very close runner-up position. Distance sons and daughters, who continuously mediate the guilt of left behind family, take the cake and win the biggest slice of The Mediating Anxious Feelings Pie.

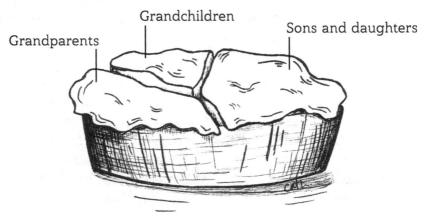

The Mediating Anxious Feelings Pie

Their emotions ruminate, fester and never go away and only increase as their parents age. Sick and/or dying family living afar raise levels of anxiety and guilt to an all-time high from which there is no escape.

In short, distance family worry also.

Third Culture Kids (TCKs)

"Globalization has given many of us unparalleled opportunities to work, travel, fall in love, and raise kids all over the world. But it has made being a teen more complicated than ever. Imagine having to discover your identity and place in the world when you keep having to move communities, your parents are from different backgrounds, you're exposed to multiple cultures daily or faced with challenges such as global warming and pandemics."
Dr Anisha Abraham, *Raising Global Teens*

When families move overseas, or children are born overseas, it doesn't take long before the parents (distance sons and daughters) realise their children have an altered identity from their own. Yes, the children's home or passport country is a part of them (culture number one) plus they are part of the country they are currently living in (culture number two). Additionally, these children are becoming global citizens: the world of globalisation and mobility is their third culture.

Third Culture Kids, the enduring book by David C. Pollock, Ruth E. Van Reken and Michael V. Pollock, is onto its third edition. As the years have passed since the 1999 first edition written by Van Reken with Michael Pollock's late father, David, they have moved from historical discussions of expat children attending boarding schools located in the home country, to the current global business of International Schools situated just down the road.

Oftentimes the distance family doesn't realise it is possible to own these multiple identities, but when the term *Third Culture*

Kid is explained to them it's like a lightbulb has been turned on. Clarity appears and overnight the children and their parents begin to understand why these children are neither one, nor the other.

TCKs are most at home in a global world crammed jammed full of diverse peoples and diverse places. Eventual repatriation, to the home of their parents (and grandparents), for example, can be traumatic, especially if that destination is primarily monocultural and they have been used to multicultural environments. While their parents are likely revelling in being back home, the children are fish out of water. When they begin school or university they naturally gravitate to any foreign-looking young person who might deliver the diversity they yearn for.

TCKs might be a foreign concept to Distance Grandparents; however, I recommend becoming aware of this terminology. Each day your grandchildren are living overseas, their identity is changing - slowly, but surely, they are becoming Third Culture Kids.

What it means for the Distance Grandparents is their distance grandchildren are not *all* American, or *all* English or *all* Australian or whatever nationality the grandparents are. They have absorbed and embraced different customs and cultures and may not act and be like the other grandchildren (their cousins) at home. Some Distance Grandparents adjust better than others to having a globally diverse family. It can be confronting, foreign and challenging.

In short, your distance grandchildren are different from your local grandkids. Additionally, the distance grandchildren's parents, while coping with a myriad of cultural changes themselves, are continuously monitoring their children to ensure they are thriving wherever they land.

Work and Careers Matter a Lot

Generation X and Generation Y distance sons and daughters and Generation Z grandchildren are the most educated generations on the planet and in the workforce. Baby Boomers (Distance Grandparents), as a generation, never achieved the same educational achievements while gender roles were - and often still remain - more defined for this older age group.

The by-product of this higher education and all it took in time, energy and money has resulted in career paths and professional development being of paramount importance for distance sons, daughters and grandchildren. Talk of career strategy and prospects is constant. They are continuously looking out for the next move: the next advancing opportunity.

Two situations often crop up that impact these attitudes and the identity of distance sons, daughters and grandchildren.

First, one half of a couple will generally be following the other, the one whose career move assignment initiated the relocation. The latter is nearly always a male. The non-employed other half (mainly a woman) often feels rudderless, asking themselves, *What am I going to do?* The answer to this question is complex and not necessarily obvious, let alone what might appeal.

Second, starting a family, though a welcomed milestone, also upsets career plans. Few distance family households escape this dilemma. Financial strains, gender role inequality and identity issues take centre stage as the parents are simultaneously raising their child or children.

Carine Bormans and Marie Geukens in *Expat Partner* are sympathetic to these scenarios. They claim there are multiple solutions for multiple situations and keeping an open mind to other ways of achieving professional development is the key.

In short, careers, jobs and professional development matter to distance sons, daughters and grandchildren - more than they might have in the past for the parents and grandparents.

What and Where is Home?

As time passes the meaning of home for distance family evolves, reshapes and transforms. Just because the grandparents might believe their home location is best, our distance children and grandchildren do not automatically feel the same way.

Each trip home for them comes with a changing level of connectedness and wavering expectations. They are a changed person from the last visit and they are a changed person on consequent visits. Their passport indicates they are nationals but this may not mirror their identity.

Over time, home can for some become a confronting, foreign destination of apprehension.

In short, home for distance family doesn't necessarily mean what their parents might think it means.

It is Hard for Our Distance Family to Share Their World and Most Times... No One Back Home is Interested

Just as Distance Grandparents experience a sense of loneliness, it can be the same for distance sons, daughters and grandchildren, more especially when they visit home. Their current overseas home location forms part of their identity; however, there is little interest from those at home about their new life.

Their foreign world is brushed over by family and friends, in favour of local topics, relevant to the in-country family and friends. It is not that they don't care, they simply don't get *why* the distance family live where they live and *why* they don't want to go back home. If local family and friends haven't travelled much themselves, the situation for the visiting family can be even more problematic. A degree of ignorance about the rest of the world can exist.

In short, visiting distance sons, daughters and grandchildren are wise to leave talk of their current home safely stored in an imaginary corner of the Airport Baggage Claim, to be later reclaimed when they board their return flight.

After this sneak preview of the book series let's come back to the job in hand and ask the question, "How is Distance Grandparenting for you?"

UNPACKING GRANDPARENTING AND DISTANCE GRANDPARENTING

"Becoming a grandmother these days does not mean packing up your former life and settling down to your declining years. On the contrary. Today our expectations of grandmothers [and grandfathers] and what they do are completely different [...] the gifts we have to offer our grandchildren are much richer and more diverse. We have so much more to draw on, and we draw on such a wide variety of personal experience [...] it enriches our grandchildren [...] since they are the beneficiaries of who and what we are."
Selma Wassermann, *The Long Distance Grandmother*

Laura Stafford from The Ohio State University describes in *Maintaining Long-Distance and Cross-Residential Relationships* the grandparent role as 'diverse, dynamic and complex' - suggesting it is neither straightforward nor plain sailing.

Her comment reminds me of Tom Hanks's reflection in the movie *Forrest Gump* when he says: "My mom always said life was like a box of chocolates. You never know what you're gonna get." This book is the chocolate box of contemporary Distance Grandparenting. Some chocolate flavours are predictable inclusions, some are less popular, while others catch you by surprise and deliver an unexpected burst of flavour.

What do Scholars and Experts Have to Say?

Janet Carsten is a Professor of Social and Cultural Anthropology at The University of Edinburgh. She has a strong interest in kinship (the study of family bonds and relationships through blood and marriage). She explains in *After Kinship* that to study families is to study kinship. Since the 1970s the nature of kinship in the West has, according to Carsten, taken on 'many new guises' to include advanced reproductive technologies and changing forms of sexuality, genders and family. Globalisation has become another guise and is central to why Distance Grandparenting is now so prevalent. German sociologists Ulrich Beck and Elisabeth Beck-Gernsheim write of the 'global chaos of love', while Professor Thomas Hylland Eriksen, an Anthropologist from Norway, explains the world is 'shrinking' and that affects how families 'family'.

Academia has its own terminology for distance families: 'transnational' families. Sociology Professor Zlatko Skrbiš from Sydney notes the term 'transnationalism' first appeared in academic debates regarding business, politics and agri-business but *not* families. It wasn't until 1990 when transnationalism *and* the family first appeared together in research. Putting this timeline into context, the 1990s were when our current crop of distance sons and daughters (now in their 30s and 40s) were babies and children. It is interesting to reflect they weren't born into a world of globalisation talk and blurred borders. Much has changed for us all in a relatively short time.

A Rite of Passage

Grandparenthood is a rite of passage even for the most tentative, reluctant participant. First-time grandparents can be as young as in their late 30s with children still at home. Others are well into their 70s when a 40-something son or daughter produces their first offspring. Some grandparents are besotted with their new role, uttering cries of 'at last'. Others are a little more hesitant when the news is announced and don't feel an immediate wash of grandparenting bliss. Some grandparents only ever have one grandchild while others go on to have a dozen or more. For them the red-letter day of first-time grandparenting blurs and sways as additional grandchildren arrive and the dynamics and nature of the role evolves further.

Few would argue when you hold a grandchild for the first time your world instantly melts. The feeling can only be described as *wondrous* when the reality sets in that a little bit of *you* has magically materialised in the form of a new human being, and this little person represents the emergence of another generation in your family.

Early November on a Friday evening my husband Clive and I disembarked from a cruise ship and flew from bustling Hong Kong to chaotic Bangkok. Thailand travel guides state November is the best time to visit - 'cool and temperate' they say. But for us, Bangkok felt like its normal hot and steamy self.

We stood in the jam-packed airporter train heading to a central station, with suitcases wedged in so they wouldn't go for a scoot. Eventually we found our American expat son-in-law buried in the moving crowd at the station and together we tackled the MRT, Bangkok's metro, for the next leg. Later we stood precariously on the road, a short distance from the curb, vigorously hailing a cab for the final kilometre or so. Cars, motorbikes and mayhem passed dangerously close. The humidity was relentless. Eventually we caught the eye of a driver whose taxi had a glowing red vacant sign. We piled in and breathed a deep sigh of relief.

As we drove into the familiar guarded apartment complex, a feeling of serenity and calm washed over us like water from a luxury rain shower head. We had arrived at what I will later refer to as one of our *places* of Distance Grandparenting.

When I walked into the ground floor apartment, my daughter wasn't there. "Lucy must be outside in the communal garden," I said to my husband. In the next room, a tiny, six-week-old bundle lay in a bassinette, hovered over by an unfamiliar local nanny, bowing to me with her eyes lowered. I sort of nodded and smiled in a confused manner, all the while berating myself for my lack of instinctive cultural etiquette. My mind was focused elsewhere and started racing. *I need to find my daughter. She would want to witness this moment.*

Lucy was found, and we tiptoed into the bedroom and she gently picked up bubs and placed him in my arms. I will never forget my first hug - no one could hold back the tears.

> **“ I will never forget my first hug -
> no one could hold back the tears. ”**

Contemporary Grandparenthood

Contemporary grandparents are different from the grandparents they knew as a child. Barbara Waxman, a Gerontology Coach and advocate for ageing, describes in an article on ageism how our increased life span is the 'demographic gift of the 21st century'. Today grandparents are active and healthy, and remain so for longer, enabling them to be more involved in the lives of their grandchildren. Active, hands-on grandparents are now considered the norm. Therefore, if children and grandchild move far away, the grandparents cannot perform a socially accepted norm - and that creates a void.

> "Grandchildren need to be around the older generation that gives them utter love and acceptance and doesn't judge them. It is very important for children."
>
> Peggy Fisher (East Coast U.S.A./Germany)

> "Grandparents are important as role models, they love them unconditionally, they can hang out with them and tell things to them - they are real people. Distance familying disrupts the ease of that relationship when it can only be enacted via a screen."
>
> Jill (N.Z./England)

Somewhere along the journey of parenthood, Distance Grandparents discover that their imagination of how things would be when grandkids arrive is no longer the reality. For many, it's a tough assignment.

Grandmothers versus grandfathers?

There is a generally accepted belief grandmothers do more grandparenting then grandfathers. I have seen plenty of evidence of this; however, I want to put in a good word for Distance Grandfathers. They may not do as much grandparenting but they are proactive in the background.

While husbands are often guilty of switching off from their wife's emotional rants and raves, this is not the case in face-to-face discussions regarding their distance middle generation children and distance grandchildren. Grandfathers have thoughts, feelings and opinions and don't disappear into their cave or shed or head to the pub when the topic is raised. When the situation is right, they have plenty to say and perform their roles well.

Baby Boomer Distance Grandparents have parented during an era when gender roles tended to be more defined than they are these days, and this affects the way we grandparent. Distance Grandparent couples tend to distance family as a team as they understand how the other feels. The presence of their likeminded other half is of huge emotional support. It is all about what works best for each grandparent couple.

Later, I discuss Distance Grandmothers who travel by themselves to support their distance family and it is easy to overlook, on these occasions, the contribution of the Distance Grandfather. The men's support is crucial and sometimes they are still working to help pay for the trip. The men are accustomed to having their wives around so fending for themselves for a few weeks in an empty house isn't always their idea of fun.

Single Distance Grandparents

Single, divorced and widowed Distance Grandparents do not have the support of a partner. Without a doubt, their journey is a lonelier one and, most of the time, the distance families realise this. These grandparents not only experience the loneliness of not having their child and grandchildren to hand, but they also have no one at home to process and de-brief with as they navigate the role. Financially it is all up to them. Being a single Distance Grandparent never stops being a tough gig.

Statistics

Distance Grandparents rarely feature in census statistics anywhere - they're an under-the-radar slice of any country's population.

The only statistic I have ever gleaned was reported in a 2010 New Zealand government publication titled *Changing* and authored by Anne Kerslake Hendricks from the Families Commission. This report delivered the findings of an extensive survey of New Zealand grandparents. The author, coincidentally a Distance Grandparent, confirmed that 23% of grandparents who were interviewed had grandchildren living overseas. This is very high.

The Nature of the Overseas Adventure: the Push and the Pull

When I waddled to my ante-natal check-ups, my thoughts of mobility and movement focused on a baby transitioning through the birth canal - the push and pull factors associated with migration had not entered my world. I never gave a single thought to the concept that the children I willingly carried for nine months, who kindly left me with stretch marks, would not always be at hand.

In *The Penguin Book of Migration Literature*, Dohra Ahmad explains that mobility researchers differentiate between 'push factors' (reasons why people emigrate, for example war or economic depression) and 'pull factors' (reasons why people are attracted to immigrate to a specific country, for instance employment opportunities).

The push and pull factors provide a tool to explain two things about the nature and subjects of this book:

- The Distance Grandparents who *don't* feature in this book and should be acknowledged.
- The Distance Grandparents who *do* feature.

Not featured

The following Distance Parents and Distance Grandparents don't feature in this book:

- Those from Asian countries with their strong culture of filial piety (respect and care of elders).
- Those left behind because of war, terrorism and climate change.
- Those from third-world, remittance-receiving (money sent home by migrants) nations.

Distance Grandparenting is rarely a walk in the park for any of us. However, circumstances surrounding war, terrorism, racism and culturally and economically-affected communities cannot be compared with the left-behind parents and grandparents of the Western world, as featured in this book.

Featured

The Distance Parents and Distance Grandparents featured in this book are the by-product of pull factors. Their sons and daughters have been attracted (pulled) to leave their home country for reasons of career advancement, a sense of adventure and/or love.

Within pull factor situations, our distance sons and daughters each have their own mobility story that affects their intergenerational, distance familying experience. In this book I tend to lump everyone together - but there are different sets of circumstances. Let's address them:

- **Short-term, one-off overseas contracts**
  Both the moving middle generation and the Distance Grandparents at home tend to look on this move as an adventure and both parties want to make the most of it before the assignment is over and life returns to normal back home again.

- **Continuously on-the-move (every two or three years) expats**
  These distance sons and daughters are likely from the corporate, diplomatic, military or missionary worlds. Sometimes each move is a choice; oftentimes it isn't. With each move they get better at transitioning, making new friends, adjusting to the new culture and all too soon saying their goodbyes. At first it's a novelty, but for all concerned, including the Distance Parents at home, transitioning and global transfers become the norm.

- **Migrants settled in one place**
  Ostensibly this is a permanent move but for some it doesn't start out that way. They leave home with plans of a backpacking adventure, a working holiday or a one-off, short-term assignment. Their intention is to return home, but things change. The distance son or daughter genuinely enjoys the experience, so a permanent position is acquired, a contract is extended or another offer is received.

There are other factors affecting *all* three categories:

- **Location matters**
  A cute village in Switzerland *feels* much safer to Distance Parents (and perhaps the moving middle generation) than a Third World location, where medical facilities and

personal safety may be compromised. Furthermore, this affects the willingness of Distance Grandparents to visit.

- **Where were the grandchildren born?**
  Experiences differ between grandchildren born overseas - where the grandparents have always been at a distance - and grandchildren who are born in-country and then move overseas. When grandchildren can remember living in their passport country and seeing their grandparents on a regular basis there is a degree of closeness that never leaves them and is hard to replicate from afar.

- **Remuneration**
  There exists an assumption that expats are well-rewarded financially and life is pretty comfortable. For many this is the case and they are often better off compared with how life would be back home. There's also a good proportion of distance sons and daughters living very ordinary, everyday lives on moderate salaries. Money is discussed in more detail in later chapters and affects many aspects of distance familying.

Suffice to say, due to the differing types of moves and situations of the pull factor there is no one-size-fits-all, distance familying package. Every family has its own set of circumstances and these circumstances affect the journey of each generation.

Multi-generational Distance Familying

Once you delve into the world of mobility you soon discover veteran, multi-generational expats and migrants - corporates, academics, military, missionaries, diplomats. Their parents were expats, they are expats and their children have experienced life living abroad. Is it any wonder, when these folk find themselves Distance Grandparents for the first time, that there's an element of under-the-breath, light-hearted déjà vu mutterings of 'we got what we deserved'?

> "My parents [the Distance Grandparents] knew what to expect. They had been the middle generation of a three-generational expat family. They knew what they were setting themselves up for when they took us overseas. When we were raised overseas, soaking the fire of curiosity, this is the price they have to pay."
>
> Anna Seidel (American distance daughter living in Germany)

A higher level of robust emotional resilience exists in all quarters for multi-generational distance families. They adjust and adapt more easily to their geographical separation. And what is the norm for them can horrify other grandparents.

Peggy, Anna's mother from above, recounted how - when Anna and her sister were five and six years old - she sent them as unaccompanied minors by plane from Germany to Oregon, U.S.A., to visit their grandparents. What courage that must have taken. Keeping up this grandchild/grandparent connection was an absolute priority.

Grandparents on the Move in Retirement

In North America, and the U.K. especially, it is not unusual for retirees to pack up and permanently head south to warmer climates like Florida and Spain. There can be very good reasons for these moves, but likely the left-behind family is somewhat put out - ironically in the same way Distance Grandparents can feel put out when their children first leave for overseas. These decisions are made with considerable thought.

"Fourteen years ago we moved from New Zealand to Australia to be closer to our family and grandchildren. I was the one who wanted to move. My husband agreed to leave behind a lifestyle that suited him and catered for his many interests.

As the years passed we were there in Australia when milestones happened. We watched the boys playing sports and attended special functions. But, as the grandchildren grew we saw less of them; their family lives became organised with sport, homework and friends. Visits to our home decreased - we understood - a busy family with just a lack of time.

Recently we made the decision to return to live in our home country, New Zealand, where my husband would live more comfortably away from the heat and humidity which he was finding hard.

My Brisbane family was shocked, even angry, that we chose to make this move. They were disappointed we had chosen to distance ourselves from them. They couldn't understand at all. We departed not knowing how much we had upset them.

I was torn between my family and the needs of my husband who was now in his 70s. The Australian heat exhausted him and he missed all that New Zealand offered. I owed it to him to return.

It's been a year and I have seen our children and grandchildren once only, but with Skype and Messenger, we keep in regular contact. One day they will visit with their friends and partners and enjoy the beach life we now enjoy.

Although the decision to return to New Zealand meant leaving my children and grandchildren in Australia, it was the right one for us in our retirement years. Was it selfish? I have sometimes wondered but deep down I don't believe so, because fifty years ago we moved away from our parents and close family to begin our married lives. Our grandchildren will have the same freedom, without guilt, hopefully having freedom to be who they are."
Glennis Annie Browne - author (N.Z./Australia and Indonesia)

Communication Studies Professor Emeritus Stephen Banks from Idaho travelled to an expatriate retirement colony in Mexico to interview North American grandparents who had chosen to move south, oftentimes away from family who previously had lived nearby. Most of his research participants remained positive about their Distance Grandparenting role. A small group, however, was somewhat disconnected from their distance family, and three themes appeared. First, the distance enabled better control over timing and duration of contact with their grandchildren. Second, it was feasible to have the grandchildren visit alone and the grandparents enjoyed the absence of mediating middle generation parents. Finally, the move south extricated themselves from excessively close or dependent relationships. This study highlights the many agendas existing for Distance Grandparents.

Retiring expat Distance Grandparents

The fascinating by-product of multi-generational distance families, as mentioned earlier, is that expats can eventually become Distance Grandparents themselves. What's more, as retirement approaches they ask the question 'where should we settle?' Home, their city, town or passport country may not feel like somewhere they want to spend their twilight years. Perhaps their own parents have now passed and connections to their home country are loose. The grandparents might be considering trying to live close to their grandchildren but the location is still shifting.

When expat Distance Grandparent Peggy (U.S.A./Germany) was deciding where to retire, her friends kept enquiring why she didn't want to go and live near her children and grandchildren. Her response was, "If you can tell me where that might be - perhaps." Her two daughters have lived in South Africa, China and California and currently live in Scotland and Germany. Peggy went on to say, "When we get a chance to see them, we are thrilled, and if we don't, we don't mope about it."

Retirement, as much as one looks forward to it, becomes a problem for these expats. Quite simply, they don't know where to live and they don't know if their expat kids will keep moving. And let's not forget issues of passports, visas, citizenship, pensions, medical benefits and so on. Retirement for seasoned-expat Distance Grandparents is a proverbial can of worms.

This book reflects more generally the thoughts of the majority of Distance Grandparents who haven't had multi-generational distance family experiences like Peggy. However, it is important to be aware that distance families come with significantly varied past and present experiences and what is the norm for some Distance Grandparents is not the norm for others.

Distance Grandparents versus Global Grandparents

Oftentimes Distance Grandparents are referred to as global grandparents. I spent time debating these two titles. I chose to embrace Distance Grandparents, rather than global grandparents, for two reasons.

First, if you live on one coast of the U.S.A. or Canada and your grandchildren live on the other you are definitely a Distance Grandparent. You might all live in the same country, but you have to cope with geographical barriers and boundaries just like globally-separated families. These grandparents need to be acknowledged in this book and shouldn't be excluded because they aren't *global* in a nationality sense.

Global sounds a little more prestigious and, yes, does remind you it comes with a certain fascination and curiosity, but the reality is the distance never goes away and no amount of global charm will offset the reality that we are *Distance* Grandparents, more than *global* grandparents.

How far is the *Distance* of Distance Grandparenting?

What qualifies a grandparent to be a Distance Grandparent? I can confirm there are no hard and fast rules.

When I conducted my university research, I decided to apply a rule that a weekend visit to family was logistically out of the question. The east coast of Australia, for example, is two hours behind New Zealand and a three-hour international flight from major New Zealand cities. To a New Zealander's way of thinking, a weekend visit to Sydney, Melbourne or Brisbane is viable. I label my Distance Grandparent friends with grandchildren in these cities *short haul* Distance Grandparents. I label grandparents with family further afield *long haul* Distance Grandparents.

Short haul grandparenting and long haul grandparenting share many of the same challenges. However, the significant difference between the two is that, finances permitting, short haul distance families *can* reasonably easily visit each other for a weekend: a valuable psychological advantage and benefit.

This book comes with no hard and fast rules about what is the *distance* of Distance Grandparenting. Whether your distance family live just a few hours' drive away or a visit involves endless hours navigating multiple flight connections, the book's messages remain the same.

The Voice of Knowing

When an American author writes a Distance Grandparenting book, most of the featured grandparents tend to be American. Likewise, when an English writer authors a similar book, many of the grandparents are from the U.K. Keeping with this trend, New Zealand grandparents often feature in this book. There is a reason why I am highlighting this.

All Distance Grandparent voices are valuable; however, the voices of New Zealand Distance Grandparents offer a particularly broad perspective to this book's conversation due to a combination of five barrier/boundary factors they *all* experience. Most Distance Grandparents from other parts of the world do not experience all five barriers. The factors are:

1. **Location on the globe**
   There is no arguing New Zealand is a long way from much of the world and you feel isolated when you live here. Sir John Key, a former New Zealand Prime Minister, once stated in a speech that our country is 'the last bus stop on the planet'. When we travel overseas, people we meet often comment how New Zealand is 'such a long way away', while we don't use the same language in reverse.

2. **Exclusive time zone**
   New Zealand sits almost exclusively in its own time zone. Time zones significantly affect the ease of distance family communication and feature frequently in ongoing chapters. A time zone map (see over) shows another couple of territories also in an exclusive time zone: India and Alaska. The bottom line is that *all* Distance Grandparents from New Zealand (and India and Alaska) must contend with time zone issues, no matter where their distance family live.

3. **Hemisphere ups and downs**
   When it is winter in the Southern Hemisphere, it is summer in the Northern Hemisphere. Likewise, the school year starts in February in New Zealand, while for much of the Northern Hemisphere it begins in August/September. The Southern Hemisphere is a calendar-year focused region, while the Northern Hemisphere's summer creates bookends to many employment contracts and educational semesters. These differences cause planning challenges, especially once grandchildren are at school and travel bookings need to focus around school terms. It isn't possible for Northern Hemisphere school-age distance grandchildren to enjoy an extended summer break in New Zealand, as it's school term time.

4. **Daylight saving**
   New Zealand, along with other countries, has the twice-

yearly adjustments for daylight saving. This can create for some a six-monthly, flip-flopping communication routine between morning/evening as the time difference changes, for example, from 11 to 13 hours. Additionally, for a few weeks during the transitional periods of March/April and September/October, when everyone is changing, confusion reigns and one is never sure who is on what time.

5. **International date line**

   The last and significant geographical factor sits alongside New Zealand's eastern border: the International Date Line. This zigzagging, 180-degree meridian imaginary line was decided upon in 1884 in Washington, D.C., at the International Meridian Conference where 26 countries attended. Its location was purposely selected due to the area's sparse population. From a Kiwi's perspective, during the few shared daylight hours of countries in the Americas, we are each on a different day of the week. When it is Sunday daytime in New Zealand, it is Saturday daytime in the Americas.

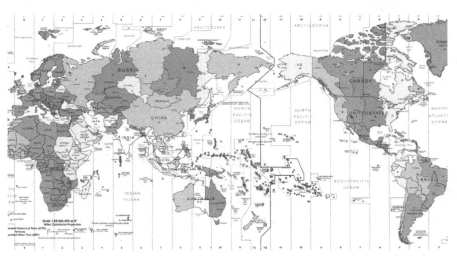

Standard time zones of the world.
Image courtesy of Wikimedia Commons.

Few other territories or nations experience *all* five factors, and an awareness of this enables Distance Grandparents from all parts of the globe to compare their lot. Perhaps some readers will discover there's a barrier or two they do not have to cope with... and that's a good thing.

My final contribution to highlighting our topsy-turvy world is an explanation of my deliberate choice of map. It will look odd to some readers who are accustomed to maps with the Americas on the left, while Africa, Europe and Asia are centre-right and New Zealand squashed into the bottom right-hand corner - or sometimes missing altogether.

During a visit to America I was once asked what route my return flight journey would take. "Do you go via Tokyo?" they said. For a moment I was speechless. *Why would you nearly double the journey time and go backwards to go forwards?* I patiently explained there are non-stop, 15-17 hour direct services to Auckland from the likes of San Francisco, Los Angeles, Houston and Chicago. I hope this map awakens another way of seeing distance.

A Grandparenting Quandary

Margaret Mahy (1936-2012) was a prolific New Zealand author of children and young adult books, which have been translated into 15 languages. (An all-time favourite is *A Lion in the Meadow.*) She was awarded New Zealand's greatest honour, the Order of Merit. The mother of two was often seen at children's events wearing a rainbow-coloured woollen wig complemented by zany, out there clothes.

Mahy's ponderings regarding grandparenthood offer wisdom, clever observations and some home truths, all from the perspective of what she, as a grandmother, both openly and secretly desired. I have included these words (below) mainly because of the last sentence. It is especially poignant in the context of Distance Grandparenting:

> "I, myself, want to be an active part of the lives of my grandchildren. I want to be part of their daily scenery and want them to be part of mine. I want them to remember me bending over their cots, mumbling as I change their napkins [diapers]. I want to praise their advances into the world, applaud their first words, tell them stories and listen to them when they begin to tell their own. I want to pin pictures especially drawn for me on my walls. **Of course, there are elements of unconscious egotism in all this, for one's family represents part of self, but self successfully set free from self - detached, launched and independently at large in the world.**"
> Margaret Mahy, *Grand Stands*

Mahy's comments left me with two thoughts:
One: as parents we want our children to be self-sufficient and independent, as this is satisfying and an outward sign of successful parenting. We are proud our children have ventured into the world, found homes in different lands and created their new lives. We enjoy, to some degree, the trappings and status of this global parental success and it can all make for captivating dinner table talk.

Two: however, is this just a convenient public persona, a cover-up for a package of circumstances Distance Parents and Distance

Grandparents would rather not exist, as they worry, *why couldn't my children be like the ones who stay home?*

Are we both proud and sad at the same time, wishing there were reins on how far away Margaret Mahy's 'at large in the world' actually is?

A good person to ask this was Jenny Gosling, widow of Peter, co-author of *How To Be A Global Grandparent.* They regularly travelled from the U.K. to Dubai, Oman, Norway and Malaysia to visit their daughter, well-known author Jo Parfitt, and her husband and two boys. The family would also visit the U.K. during the hot Middle East summers.

"Jo was busy every morning but always spent afternoons with us and took us out," she said. "Often we looked after the boys in the morning too. Yes, I admit I resented her working a bit because we had come a long way to visit her." Later Jenny admitted while sharing a gentle tear, "We were terribly proud, of course, though I am not one to crow about my children and grandchildren. It was my husband who did that! We felt and feel a strong sense of pride in what they were all doing but missed them terribly."

Jenny is not alone nursing these mixed emotions and many readers will relate to her.

KEY FINDINGS: THE *HOW IT IS*

My research findings are straightforward, while simultaneously complex. How Distance Grandparenting *is* can't be isolated and defined in a tidy, separate part of the grandparent's being. The *how it is*, is the sum of five Package Factors and six Recurring Themes.

Five Package Factors

1. **Their current personal package**
   Here, I am referring to the grandparents' ages, health, employment, marital status, financial situation, ability or desire to travel, and so forth.
2. **Their in-country family package**
   Questions need to be asked around the number and ages of the grandparents' children (middle generation) and grandchildren, as well as locations, routines of contact, obligations of caring in either direction and the quality of relationships.
3. **Their distance family package**
   The same questions as above need to be asked around the number and ages of the grandparents' children (middle generation) and grandchildren, as well as overseas locations, routines of contact, obligations of caring in either direction and the quality of relationships. Additionally, the nature of the middle generation's move (short-term, on-the-move or permanent) needs to be known.

4. **Geographical and communication barriers, restrictions and boundaries**

   Geographical boundaries are what ostensibly create the *distance* part of Distance Grandparenting - which is why talk of time zones and other communication barriers weave themselves through the book. There is no escaping from these barriers. They are understood by Distance Grandparents on an intellectual level, but also felt at a very human and emotional level.

5. **Cultural, religious and/or language issues**

   Cultural, religious and/or language issues are also important topics for gaining a full picture of Distance Grandparenting. Some families are affected more than others: there is no shortcut here.

Six Recurring Themes

1. Distance Parenting - once a parent, always a parent

This book is titled *Being a Distance Grandparent - a Book for ALL Generations*. The title Distance Grandparent automatically assumes there is a Distance *Parental* relationship present: an implied connection. One rarely hears the title Distance Parent - which comes with none of the cuteness of Distance Grandparent. However, once you are a parent, you are always a parent, and being a Distance *Parent* is critical to this discussion.

Despite the purposeful direction and title of this book, the subject of parenting never takes a back seat. Grandparents care just as much, sometimes more, about their roles as *parents* (distance or in-country) and this can sometimes be overlooked. When I wake each morning, I first wonder how my *children* are, before I think about how my *grandchildren* are. This does not lessen the value of a discussion of Distance Grandparenting - more a case of *once a parent, always a parent*.

2. The place of Distance Grandparenting is multi-sited

Anthropology Professor Edward Bruner from Chicago, who passed away in 2020 while this book was being written, talked of the continuously moving 'space' or 'place' of tourists who progress through their itinerary from one performance space to another. At the same time, Melbourne-based Professor Sarah Pink explains place as a coming together and 'entanglement' of persons, things, directions, sensations and stories.

Distance Grandparents, like Bruner's tourists, perform in and move between four places or spaces - each one overflowing with Pink's entanglement.

At any one time, Distance Grandparents may be found doing their role in one of the following places:

1. *Their empty home*
   Their empty house is one of mundane, comforting routines. The Distance Grandparents' senior years deliver an opportunity to retain a continuous sense of order, if preferred. The empty house is also the site of the spare bedroom or bedrooms: rooms that stay as is for long periods of time. Most grandparents would admit these rooms receive intermittent visits with a duster and vacuum cleaner but of course enjoy a thorough spring clean and airing when guests are expected. This empty place, their home, is one of silence: any noise is introduced by choice of the occupants.

2. *Their full home, hosting distance family*

   After a patient wait in the airport's Arrival Hall and a drive home, the Distance Grandparents' everything-in-its-place home is invaded by an excited, boisterous cacophony of chatter and suitcases infused by a jet lag haze. The new arrivals take in the somewhat familiar surroundings as regularly seen in the background of video chats. The family has arrived. Home, as the grandparents know it, temporarily evaporates.

3. *The full home of the distance son or daughter when visited by the Distance Grandparents*

   Both familiar and strange - once again, décor and life's things you normally only see on a screen can be touched and admired. On the one hand this place of Distance Grandparenting instils a feeling of relief knowing you have arrived and the flight/ flights are over. You aren't going anywhere for a bit. On the other hand, grandparents may experience an overwhelming urge to hide before they feel they can truly face the world. Thoughts of, *Beam me up, Scotty*. There can be the overwhelming need for a familiar cup of tea, a shower or an undisturbed lengthy sit on the toilet. For others, totally unpacking is a priority or sourcing out the Wi-Fi code and reconnecting again. While most of us fall into one of these categories, there are of course those zealous grandparents who just want to get on the floor and play. I admit I am not one of them. "Please may I have a shower and where is the guest hairdryer I bought last time and purposely left behind?"

4. *The virtual home: the co-presence of cyberspace*

   This is where we spend most of our time as Distance Grandparents and it dominates the next chapter, *Communication Routines*. Bonds and relationships are poked at, prodded, patted, stroked and nourished... as best as you can manage, given the barriers and boundaries, all the while supported by the best of intentions from both sides.

3. Loneliness is ever-present

Distance Grandparenting (and Distance Parenting) can, from time to time, be a lonely experience. I would describe this loneliness as *emotions on a shelf* - there is little one can do about it, so let's just shelve them.

There is the obvious loneliness of not having all one's family near - that's a given.

Women struggling with infertility experience the loneliness of their circumstances when they see their friends having babies. The sight of local grandparent friends with their grandchildren can never match the empty feelings of the younger women, but there is a sliver of similarity. For example, I am a pretty stoic grandmother, most of the time. You won't find me pining for the little ones from afar, making those around me feel uncomfortable. However, there is one place where I am not so upbeat. At the end of each church service our priest welcomes all small children to receive a blessing. With gay abandon little ones waddle, run and skip up the aisle. Occasionally I see a grandparent I know, carrying or accompanying an unfamiliar child or two. I think to myself, *the grandkids are in town*. I quietly melt in my seat feeling very alone.

Visiting family overseas can be both crowded and lonely. You're mixing in your children's world and you're pleased to be there but culturally or linguistically it can be an isolating place. Maybe the visit is for the occasion of an important family milestone, like a wedding. You might be the *only* distance family there - it can happen. You are on show, stand out in the crowd and sound different. What's more, when you return home there is no one to share the memories with: you're in another lonely place.

Even the temporary presence of visiting family can ironically create a form of isolation and loneliness. When I have overseas family visit, my local friends and extended relatives, showing lots of consideration and knowing how precious the time is with our visiting family, give us a wide berth. The phone does not ring, there are no dinner invitations or texts asking if I feel like a walk. For a few days or a week or two we are figuratively in a bubble of distance-family-presence, supported by the kindness and consideration of our local family and friends who, over time, have acquired an appreciation of our family package. When they see a Facebook airport departure post, the phone begins to ring again.

4. Alone time - the greatest gift

Distance family connections, whether online or in-person, tend to be dominated by group settings. This is not a negative, but Distance Grandparents also hungrily cherish opportunities for alone time with *individual* distance family members.

During visits, alone time might involve everyday routine outings: simply a drive in the car with your daughter-in-law, a coffee stop with your son, a supermarket visit with a teenage grandchild or a walk down the road with a grandchild to the playground. Gone, temporarily, are the dynamics of the ever-present group situations and you are magically transported to a cherished, albeit temporary, bubble of intimacy. Despite technology, alone time can sometimes feel like the screen has disappeared because it can deliver the opportunity for deeper connections, which I will talk of in the next chapter, *Communication Routines*.

Valerie (Wales/Australia) recalled during her last visit to Australia she slept on the sofa bed in the lounge. There was never a chance for a sleep-in; however, she treasured the quiet moments when the grandchildren would sit and chat with her on the sofa as they got ready for school in the morning - precious memories.

"When we went to [distance] Simon's high school graduation ceremonies, he was given only two tickets for the special formal tea and chose, above all others, to invite his grandparents. Such a reward is only comparable to arriving at the gates of heaven."
Selma Wassermann, *The Long Distance Grandmother*

As each generation transitions, alone time can take on a new form and sometimes generate unexpected emotions. For example, a distance grandchild who used to drag their visiting grandparents around fun parks, matures, and on a later visit is enthused about a city outing to the theatre. Afterwards, the grandchild may realise they have grown up since their grandparents last visited. They're transitioning from a child to an adult relationship with their Distance Grandparents. This relational change is also experienced by the grandparents.

Shona and Brian (N.Z./Scotland) had a precious, two-day visit one Christmas from their four young adult grandchildren - the first for many years. Shona said, "I guess we learnt a lot about them in that time and especially the eldest, John, who is now about 24. He and I walked and walked and talked and talked and he said, 'I realise education is very important, but not as important as communication' and I said amen to that. We fell in love with John all over again. He was fabulous."

Rhonda and Colin (N.Z./Germany) talked of the visits by their distance family to New Zealand and of their craving for alone time. When their son came with his teenage children, but not his wife, the children monopolised his attention and the grandparents never had a quiet moment with him. When the son came on another visit, this time with his wife and no children, the grandparents were pleased to see the couple spend time together - but once again, there was little one-on-one time with their son. Rhonda and Colin would describe alone time for them as about having their son 'all to themselves'.

"We found as daughters our relationship with our mum deepened as adult to adult when we had more alone times with her."

Rhoda Bangerter, distance daughter in Switzerland with mother in the U.K.

Sometimes, it is in the alone time the truth comes out, as Mary (N.Z./England) discovered: "I know my son gave the impression his marriage was happy and healthy for several years - before he sat down and told me how he really felt and enrolled my emotional support."

These transitional, sometimes awakening experiences can take relationships, despite the distance, to a whole new level. Buzzing feelings of gratitude, elation and intense closeness are not over-the-top descriptions for the emotions experienced. Alone time *is* the greatest gift.

5. The in-country family matter

In my research of Distance Grandparenting I have rarely seen mention of the in-country family - the children (siblings) who remained home. It is as though they don't exist. If you ask the question 'How is Distance Grandparenting for you?' the discussion of their in-country family is upfront, evident and can't be brushed aside. By way of example, when I sat down with Rhonda and Colin (N.Z./Germany) I was presented with a carefully typewritten document: a helpful family-tree checklist reminder of names, birth dates, home locations and other details of both the distance *and* in-country family. Parents do not tidily separate their near and far children.

A visit with another couple, Jack and Karen (N.Z./England), solidified my thoughts here. Jack, father of seven, made me think when he said, "Well, I feel like a bit of a fraud [as an interviewee] because we've only got two [distance grandchildren]. We have got 12 grandchildren [altogether] and only two overseas. As we jokingly said, when we went through English customs a year ago [...] The guy was stamping our passports and we said we were here to see our grandchildren and the guy said it must be very hard [...] travelling all this way. 'Oh, we have another nine at home' [and one on the way]. So sure... we miss the ones in England but when we want a dose of it [grandparenthood], we can't have any sort of gathering here without at least five in Auckland, and often there are more. So, I'm not sure what to say [at this interview]. We miss the two in London, but we've now got so many [here]. Is that terrible?" Distance Grandparenting is just one aspect of the balancing act of *doing family* and cannot be isolated from what's happening at home.

In-country family will feature further in this book.

6. Change is a constant companion

Distance Grandparenting regularly evolves, flip-flops and transitions as life and whatever the world throws at it causes constant change. Nothing stays the same for long and at times our worlds can feel like an emotional yo-yo - much of it beyond our control. Sometimes comments were shared making me recall a past conversation with the same person, about the same subject, and I realised how they *now* view and cope with Distance Grandparenting has changed, yet again.

For example, the tearful grandparents I met during a couple of my interviews could just as likely be upbeat the next day, and the ones who were robust and stoic could easily appear a little melancholic another time. For me, there are times when Distance Grandparenting is not an issue and the next day, something happens, or there is a problem on the other side of the world, and it all changes.

When family dynamics are on the table and distance is added to the equation, every family can be just one Skype call away from a new regime, some difficult words or a crisis of sorts.

Pulling these factors and themes together, I argue that how Distance Grandparenting *is*, at any given moment, for each and every Distance Grandparent, can be complex and unpredictable. It's an ever-changing balancing act of relationships, emotions, communication routines, loss, acceptance, being there and a plethora of practical issues, all fused around their current personal situation, their in-country family package, their distance family package, geographical barriers and cultural, religious and/or language issues.

Despite the apparent complexity of these findings, I am pleased to report the Distance Grandparents featured in this book are not complicated people. They are ordinary folk who remain generally upbeat, while simultaneously working on accepting and adjusting to the ups and downs and the pros and cons of their dispersed family role.

The Distance Family Thinking Pie: How Big is Your Slice?

The Distance Family Thinking Pie is a symbolic reminder that each generation thinks about each other according to their own set of scales. The slices of thinking vary in size.

A healthy understanding of The Distance Family Thinking Pie delivers realistic expectations of each generation. This in turn contributes to emotionally resilient distance family relationships.

Let's consider how The Distance Family Thinking Pie is divided between the generations.

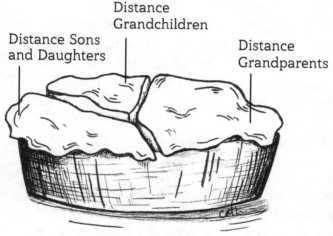

The Distance Family Thinking Pie

Distance Grandparents

Distance Grandparents consume the biggest slice of The Distance Family Thinking Pie. They think about their distance children most, followed closely by thoughts of their distance grandchildren. They worry, they grieve, they feel the void: their distance family is constantly on their minds. When they wake up each morning one of their first thoughts will be, *are there any messages overnight from the kids*?

Distance sons and daughters

Distance sons and daughters think about their Distance Parents often, but not as frequently as their parents think about them in reverse. Theirs is a middle-size slice. Keeping with the same example, first thing in the morning, distance sons and daughters have a full to-do list. They don't necessarily have time to ponder about their parents as they are rushing to get on with the day. There is only so much space, or 'bandwidth', as they would describe it.

The only time the size of the slice of The Distance Family Thinking Pie increases for the sons and daughters is when perhaps a parent is unwell and uncertainty about their future is a lingering concern. It is then the slice sizes of The Distance Family Thinking Pie are adjusted.

Distance grandchildren

Distance grandchildren consume the smallest slice of The Distance Family Thinking Pie. Most distance grandchildren don't think about their Distance Grandparents much, but it doesn't mean they don't care. Let's face it, most of us didn't think about our grandparents much at the same age. Their brain space focuses on many other things and that's perfectly normal. Once again there are exceptions to the rule. I have come across grandchildren, more especially those who grew up geographically close to their grandparents and later moved away, who are very devoted to their Distance Grandparents. They are constantly thinking about them. However, they are the exception.

Pie reflections

The purpose of talking about The Distance Family Thinking Pie is in no way to critique each generation's efforts. It is there for one purpose only: to highlight the reality that the quantity of distance family thinking varies between generations. This provides a context for realistic expectations of each other.

There is no right or wrong answer about what is the appropriate amount of thinking to dedicate to your distance family. If the family is functioning well and everyone's needs are being met as best they can be, that's an excellent result. However, if distance families are not functioning so well it might be the portioning up of The Distance Family Thinking Pie isn't quite right. Reducing your expectations of the other generations will likely find you thinking less about what you have no control over.

COMMUNICATION ROUTINES

"Grandparents today are too often much more remote geographically, and for some, the physical distance understandably plays havoc with opportunities for closer emotional connections [...] And such a set of physical estrangements of parents from parents of parents is very much an accepted part of our complex, sophisticated, career-led, urban lives."
Selma Wassermann, *The Long Distance Grandmother*

An outsider's viewpoint of Distance Grandparenting is often summed up in a well-meaning, candid remark such as 'Well, there's always Skype' - as if it were the magical solution to keeping in touch. But as we all know, there is so much more to Distance Grandparenting than the miracles of digital communication.

Looking Back

Veteran Distance Grandparents still remember the days of expensive phone calls. A $100 charge for a Christmas Day chat wasn't unusual. The telephone was permanently wired to the wall and the earpiece was passed from ear to ear. Digital communication has undoubtedly transformed distance family communication in recent years and there is much to be grateful for.

To demonstrate how rapidly our engagement with communication has changed, I will share a story from my research. When doing some groundwork I was attracted to a 2007 article analysing Distance Grandparent/grandchild usage of three communication mediums: face-to-face, telephone and email. It wasn't until I properly read the article I realised 'face-to-face' didn't mean video communication, which I had assumed. It meant *in the flesh*. Video communication, so commonplace today, was not on a publisher's radar in 2007. Skype, for example, one of the first video platforms to evolve, was only created in 2003 and remained in its infancy for some time.

A lot has changed in a very short time. However, despite all the mind-boggling communication advancements available to us, connecting with distance family is still not as simple as dialling up whenever you feel like a chat. When I chat with Distance Grandparents, their communication routines are consistently a much talked-about subject and often the first topic they raise. But before we start on this important aspect of day-to-day distance familying, let's begin with an analogy to put the digital communication part of distance familying into perspective.

Hanging Out in the Foyer: a Makeshift Place of Virtual Intimacy

When distance families communicate digitally, it's like attending the theatre but never leaving the foyer. Digital communication is the foyer of the most revered distance family performance: the prized and treasured, physical, face-to-face visits full of sights, sounds, touch and smells. Foyers are the place of making do with what we've got. They can *also* be the place of making the most of what's available to us.

Foyers *can* be fun: they can offer envied ice creams, popcorn, pizza, a glass of wine, a craft beer, your favourite coffee or a nice cup of tea, accompanied by a slice of decadent cake.

Foyers can be places of celebration: a birthday occasion, recognition of an achievement, a place of jubilation with balloons and streamers.

Foyers are also the place of the mundane: ordinary, predictable connections - nothing startling, nothing untoward - the stuff of day-to-day.

And then there's the awkward friend who appears unexpectedly in the foyer, insisting on joining in. Your anticipated private space of connection is breached and invaded.

At the end of the performance, foyers can be the quiet place of mixed emotions or elation, laughter, shouts of glee, reminiscing, unanswered questions and discussions about the plot.

Likewise, foyers are the place of pretending, holding back tears and searching for a degree of decorum, reaching for your sunglasses to hide your upset.

Sometimes the foyer turns to custard. There is an unexpected power cut, your phone battery is flat or the Wi-Fi is down. Occasionally you never actually make it to the foyer - a meeting drags on, the traffic is bad, you can't find a parking space, the train is late, or heaven forbid you dash in to find you've got the wrong day.

The reality of our shared, in-between, theatre-going distance familying worlds is *most* of the time we hang out in the foyer... the digital terms... the *cloud*... a place of anticipation... a place of makeshift virtual intimacy.

Barriers and Boundaries

First, I will address the existing barriers and boundaries to distance family communication. These fall into three categories:

1. Geographical
2. Digital: a smorgasbord of choice (or flux)
3. People

1. Barriers and boundaries: geographical

In *Unpacking Grandparenting and Distance Grandparenting*, when discussing *The Voice of Knowing* I spoke of geographical boundaries imposed on distance families, depending on where they live, which were:

1. Time zones
2. Hemisphere/seasonal variations
3. Daylight saving
4. International date line

These factors are coped with, day in, day out. They never go away and feature in many stories from grandparents.

Time zones
Of all the barriers requiring managing, time zones cause the most havoc and deserve greater acknowledgement. Time zones affect so much of how the world interacts, however little is written about them. A *Google Scholar* search of *time zones*, along with *family communication*, reveals few results. This is surprising considering the explosive growth of globalisation and the significant impact time zones have on the distance family communication.

Beijing-based communications and technologies researcher Xiang Cao offers the most relevant commentary and mirrors much of my own findings. Cao engages at a genuinely human level, talking about the sensitivity and awareness of time zones and how family values are affected by time zones. Distance Grandparents use similar language to his when describing times zones - words like troublesome, restrictive, stubborn and hampering spontaneity.

Importantly, not all distance families are affected by time zones. Grandparents living in Western Australia are in the same time zone as family who live in China, the Philippines, Singapore, Hong Kong, Taiwan, Indonesia and parts of Russia. Similarly, the United Kingdom is only an hour different from South Africa, and East Coast America is in the same time zone, or an hour or so different, as most of South America.

Distance families therefore land in one of two different time zone camps:

1. Time zone unaffected, or minimally affected
2. Time zone significantly affected

Allowing for the fact time zones are the most troublesome barrier, it is fair to say distance familying experiences vary markedly between the time-zone-affected and time-zone-unaffected: the ease of communicating is poles apart (excuse the pun). If you have never lived with a significant time zone difference between family, it is hard to appreciate how it interferes with the frequency and quality of meaningful connections.

Synchronicity
The main challenge time zones impose is the resulting small window of opportunity available for synchronised connections.

My daughter, Lucy, works full-time and our grandsons are in school and daycare. The only time it is both the weekend daytime in the U.S.A. and also the weekend daytime in New Zealand, are a few hours on our Sunday morning. Should this clash with other plans, at either end, then it's another week before a family chat is possible.

Maureen (N.Z./East Coast U.S.) explained. "It is not as easy to communicate when you feel like it. The time zone thing is the hardest thing because there are times when you think I just want to have a chat *now*. I just want to talk about whatever and you realise this isn't going to work. They're asleep, or whatever." Maureen went on to explain that when a call is finally synchronised, she might not want to talk about whatever it was anymore. "And so, I sort of feel cheated. I haven't been able to do that - darn. It's the time-zone thing again."

This part of Distance Grandparenting makes *every minute* of connection so precious. It brings back those panic feelings from decades ago, which older grandparents remember, of expensive phone calls and not wanting to waste a minute. When a FaceTime or Skype call chimes, Distance Grandparents stop everything in the same way they would have for an international phone call years ago. They rarely say 'I'll ring you back' because now, not in half an hour, is likely the only time on offer.

All the technology in the world is of no value if one party is asleep when the other is awake. Affected Distance Grandparents reluctantly accept time zones and problems achieving synchronicity are necessary evils - things you must work around. Acceptance of these is a basic given for distance families.

Cao sums up the challenges of time zones as follows:

> *"Despite the fast advances in communication technology, time difference remains one of the few challenges in telecommunications that will likely never be truly "solved" [...] Therefore, understanding the role of the time difference in connecting families can be regarded as both a timeless and a timely thesis [...]"*
> Xiang Cao, *Connecting Families*

In a reflective afterthought, Cao asserts zone distances pose *more* challenges than geographical distances for remote families. On a day-to-day basis this is valid. However, it is important to acknowledge when long-distance travel becomes a physical and/or financial impossibility for some, at least time zone differences remain a constant and can be worked around as best as can be if the desire from both sides to communicate is strong enough.

2. Barriers and boundaries: a digital smorgasbord of choice and flux

Gone are the days of us all having just a landline telephone, everyone being on the same page and, in some respects, equal in their status and ability to connect. Nowadays, real-time communication is experienced through multiple digital platforms, which can unsettle, disrupt and unnecessarily complicate some distance family relationships.

'Polymedia' is a term applied in the context of distance family communication - Anthropologists Mirca Madianou and Daniel Miller explain the Greek word *poly* means *many*. The scholars argue in their cultural studies journal article that this term has emerged as a way to describe and understand the explosive array of communication opportunities available. No longer is cost a factor to keeping in touch, rather it is *which* platform, or platforms, work best at both emotional and functional levels for the distance family.

The Distance Grandparents I've met use a mix of applications and platforms including FaceTime, Skype, Facebook Messenger, WhatsApp, email and text. There is little to be gained by singling out one platform over another because technology is constantly evolving. My commentary will be general.

Furthermore, I have noticed grandparents can get confused about terminology. Often the word Skype is used when the platform is perhaps FaceTime. It's the same way we would say 'we're taking an Uber' when in fact it's a different brand. What devices grandparents own and which platforms they use matters little to Distance Grandparents - as long as they work.

3. Barriers and boundaries: people

Three barriers exist at a very human level in the form of:

1. **Availability**
2. **Ability**
3. **Desire**

... and these barriers vary with each generation.

Toddlers
Availability is an issue due to daytime naps and early bedtimes. **Ability** is limited and most efforts tend to be hit-and-miss. There is no other way to describe it and a lot of the time it is a miss. Patience, creativity and energy are required from all sides.

"[...] in fact there are two conversations getting in the way of each other. And I get pretty frustrated because we blokes, we like our rational, orderly conversations, so my earnest questions get swallowed up with this kind of baby dialogue."

Ken (N.Z./England)

"So, when they are feeding Alice at 6 o'clock-ish they might ring me while she is in her highchair because she can't move. My daughter-in-law holds the phone."

Maureen (N.Z./East Coast U.S.)

A toddler's **desire** is hit and miss also. There is no budging a two-year-old who defiantly shouts 'no' when given an opportunity to chat with Nana and Grandad - you cannot take it personally. Intentionality (a commitment to making it work) from all adults involved with toddler communication is a helpful ingredient but not one that's necessarily easy to deliver.

Younger children
Ability and **desire** to connect for younger children evolves and changes while **availability** improves a little. Younger children do not have daytime naps but are at school or daycare and still need to be in bed reasonably early. Add daylight saving into the mix and New Zealand grandparents, for example, with small grandchildren in the U.K. conduct a flip-flopping routine, alternating every six months from communicating first thing in their morning to communicating in their evening, as the difference changes from 11 to 13 hours.

Jim and Rebecca (N.Z./England) illustrated this well. They treasured their regular before-school sessions with their four-year-old granddaughter in England. "She has had breakfast, and she is in her school uniform," Rebecca said. They are babysitting from afar while their son is busy doing something else in the house and their daughter-in-law has already left for work. "Actually, it is very precious time. We interact almost as if she is here," Jim recounts. A few months later when I asked after their granddaughter, Rebecca reported the English weekday morning routine had changed. Their granddaughter was now out of the door just after 7 am with Mum, and there was no time for chats. Due to early bedtime and a recent daylight-saving change, calls were now restricted to weekends only: change is a constant companion for Distance Grandparents.

Younger children's **ability** to communicate improves markedly. By four years of age it's possible to have civilised conversations and the transition is exciting to experience, even from afar. Hemisphere differences start to become understood, which are fun to chat about and add a new, relatable dimension to the relationship. They notice the difference between night and day and I have been asked if I am cold because I had a jumper on when my Northern Hemisphere grandsons were in T-shirts.

Desire can fluctuate but most times younger children are willing. Sometimes they don't feel like chatting but they don't want to hurt Nana or Grandad.

"It is up to the parents to encourage children to talk to the grandparents otherwise they grow up and don't know their grandparents. This is very important. Later they grow up, they don't have time for you. But it is good they know they have a grandmother who prays for them. I told William [grandson in America], 'Grandma loves you very much and Grandma prays for you every day.'"
Hannah (England/Switzerland and U.S.A.)

Teenagers and young adults: take the accelerator off your expectations

Older children and young adults have more freedom to connect but grandparents are often not their priority. **Availability**, **ability** and **desire** are on a different plane. As Selma Wassermann explains in *The Long Distance Grandmother*, "[...] much competes for their attention." This is one of those occasions when the Distance Grandparents are forced to sit back, not make a fuss and accept what is. It is good to remember if the same grandchildren lived down the road, likely we might not hear from them much either - **availability**, **ability** and **desire** to connect would still be issues.

Valerie (Wales/Australia) explained a few years ago one of her distance twin grandsons once commented he missed Valerie too much to talk with her and that hit her. Nowadays they are grown-up 16-year-olds who cruise past the screen calling out to Grandma 'how are you?' and not wanting to chat that much. Valerie tells her distance daughter not to force them to talk with her. Valerie has accepted the current regime and believes she shouldn't push it. In contrast though, her 18-year-old granddaughter regularly pours her heart out to Valerie and happily shares her world.

As a Distance Grandparent of older grandchildren, I remain cautious about reaching out to become friends with them on social media platforms. It is a wait-to-be-asked scenario. One of the greatest gifts a teenage grandchild from afar can give their Distance Grandparent is their email address and/or mobile number. My husband and I have experienced this. It feels like you have been given a global treasure.

Colin (N.Z./Germany) wanted to be the one to email one adult granddaughter. She is his responsibility, and this relationship is special to him. However, her email responses are always addressed to Grandad *and* Grandma, which is appreciated by them both.

If you have invested time with the distance grandchildren when they were younger (especially in person), you will never lose those connections when they are navigating the teenage years. In fact, as Jenny Gosling explains, distance needn't adversely affect your family relationships and you can actually end up with a stronger relationship with your distance grandchildren than you have with your in-country grandchildren.

"My [adult] grandsons now live in Spain and Germany," Jenny said. "I have visited them both [...] and that helps a lot, so I can picture where they are. They tend to phone me once a month totally spontaneously for a long call and we text too. Sometimes just a 'How are you, Granny?' and I reply immediately. I think our relationships are strong and unique and I am very lucky. They sometimes video call but actually I am just as happy with voice calls, though it is lovely to see their faces. I think we have a better relationship with Jo [distance daughter] and always had good, open communication between us, sharing all the news. As a result, the boys stay in touch too and we communicate well. I think, in fact, the relationship I have with Jo's boys is stronger and deeper than the one I have with my [in-country] son's children, because we saw Jo's family for extended periods and got to look after the boys. My grandson, Josh, in Spain, called me yesterday for a long time because I had had a fall and he was worried about me. I am very lucky. They ring to tell me what they are doing and it makes me so happy they are happy. Not tinged with sadness at all. My grandchildren in the UK never telephone me, so the relationship with my expat grandchildren is even more special."

Distance sons and daughters
Availability is a constant issue for distance sons and daughters as they juggle work, family life and adjusting to their new foreign location plus allowing themselves some me-time. Multi-tasking, talking while doing something else, is common.

Ability isn't an obstacle for distance sons and daughters, but **desire** can regularly waver. Sometimes they simply don't feel like talking with home and they need to dig deep to ensure connecting is a priority.

Rhoda Bangerter, the author of *Holding The Fort Abroad*, shines another light on **ability** and **desire**. She is a distance daughter and wife of a travelling spouse with a non-family (friendly) posting. He works away from home, most of the time during which Rhoda physically parents alone. Life can be tough and she warns, "Be aware of the amount of work travel that is involved in your distance son or daughter's life or their partner's life. If parents call when the partner is away they may get a different response to calls when the partner is home. Distance sons and daughters may need more support then. Timing a visit during these periods can be nice."

Distance Grandparents

Distance Grandparents are generally more **available** and oftentimes have the freedom to schedule their worlds, creating semi-permanent time slots for Distance Grandparent communication. They **desire** to connect so making the time is a joy, not a burden.

Most Distance Grandparents possess the **ability** to connect digitally, albeit at different levels. Most are reasonably competent with technology or have achieved a level of confidence with the basics so they can function within their family units.

Grandparents who are uncomfortable with devices, other than a regular landline telephone, are less common these days. The communication experience for this small portion of distance families bears little resemblance to those of digitally-connecting families. In fact, when your own world is dominated by technology and you stumble over an old-school scenario, it can be confronting.

We had popped over to friends early Sunday evening for drinks. As we enjoyed a platter of nibbles and a glass of wine, the landline phone rang: an unusual occurrence in itself in the increasingly common, mobile-phone-dominated households. It was the host's mother calling from Germany, clocking in for her regular Sunday morning catch-up. Conscious of the importance of the call we indicated to carry on, assuming she would pick up her mobile phone, or an iPad and immediately connect back. But no, our host explained her mother didn't have the internet in her apartment and relied on cheap phone cards. "None of her neighbours trust the internet: no one in her apartment block has Wi-Fi," she said. It took a moment or two for me to recalibrate my thinking, trying to imagine a household disconnected in this way. Our host's mother is resourceful and independent with another daughter living nearby very willing to support her on any technology learning curve. But that won't be happening. What a different Distance Parenting experience she accepts by choice.

In between the *reasonably competent* and the *disconnected* is a group of Distance Grandparents and Distance Parents who struggle with technology. They *want* to connect and be part of this digital age but are constantly lost at sea in a foggy digital storm. Nothing is instinctive for them and they frequently give up, promising themselves they will try again another day. This all creates a feeling of hopelessness. During their lifetime they have been very competent in all manner of jobs and tasks but digital technology has got them beaten. This is a time when distance sons and daughters, or the in-country family, need to dig deep and be patient.

If this is a challenge for you I recommend persevering. Keep asking questions but just be sure to write the answers down creating your own instruction manual. Each time you realise a particular challenge has now become an instinctive response you can put a big tick in your manual and feel rightfully proud.

Levels of Connection

All communication is not equal. There is value in acknowledging this, as both a reality and as a situation worthy of a regular review.

Four levels of communication

Below are four levels, or types of communication existing between distance families:

1. **Light and fluffy**
   The occasional text, a random photo or video, posts on social media and online photo libraries.
2. **Day-to-day stuff**
   Updates on the day, administration emails, things to be sorted, questions needing an answer some time.
3. **Mediocre encounters**
   The video call that started with great intentions but finished all too early due to a crying child, the doorbell, a phone call, an 'I need the potty' cry - all manner of completely normal and ordinary interruptions of daily life resulting in, "We'll try another time."
4. **Rich encounters**
   Pre-booked and sometimes random group and/or one-on-one calls when all sides are primed and the time zone works. Children are fed and watered. The distance son or daughter has attended to the most urgent tasks on hand and the Distance Grandparents are poised ready, cup of tea in hand. Everyone feels comfortable and conversations flow with ease. Calls finish organically leaving everyone refreshed and rebooted, ready to function in the void - until the next time.

Seven rich encounter strategies

How would you describe your distance family communication? If your family functions well with mainly light and fluffy, then be pleased, because in the circumstances it's a good result. I expect though you would rather have a rich connection every time. If so, these strategies may help.

1. You can't ring a two-year-old
Whose job is it to initiate communication?

While you might think the responsibility for initiating communication should be 50/50, this doesn't always work best.

Distance Grandparents understand they have a responsibility to be the best communicators they can be. They will initiate communication but much of the time they leave the initiating to the middle generation, especially when young children are involved. It's not that the grandparents don't want to connect. It's more a case they know the distance son or daughter is likely busy and they want to talk - when the time is right. It's important for the middle generation sons and daughters to realise they are the ones who need to take the lead, most of the time.

2. Soft routines versus random potluck
The solution to achieving synchronicity is what Cao calls 'soft routines'. These are a pattern of communications: a time of the day and day of the week when, if all things work out, both households chat. Because the routines are soft they remain moveable and flexible. Neither side can be too rigid. There is an unspoken arrangement you will chat at this regular time. These appointments are often booked or reconfirmed by email or text.

When my daughter, Lucy, schedules video calls I am advised by a Google Calendar notification requiring me to click yes, maybe or no. Some would think this arrangement is clinical - I see it as her making parental communication a priority.

Random potluck connections occur when either party dials and hopes they have caught the other at a good time. Unscheduled calls, when they work, are a delightful bonus.

Ivan and Maureen (N.Z./East Coast U.S.A.) offered two sides to the discussion of soft routines versus random potluck calls. They have three sons and one lives overseas. Ivan frequently uses his drive time, to or from work, to ring his boys. No calls are pre-booked and he is adamant all boys should be treated equally. He has no pattern as to who he might catch up with. If the boys are busy when he phones, they will say so.

Interestingly, Maureen never rings her distance son or daughter-in-law unannounced. "I don't call my boys up because you don't know... it's probably a difficult time," she said. "They are probably this or that, and they won't be wanting their mum to call." Instead, she might email and say, "I'd like to have a chat. Let me know when it is a good time to call."

In contrast when random potluck calls occur and Distance Grandparents aren't available they are naturally very disappointed. In *Key Findings: The How It Is* I wrote of *The Distance Family Thinking Pie,* highlighting how little, or how much, each generation tends to think about each other. Now it's time for true confessions.

I don't want to waste a single random potluck call. So, when I organise my days, if there are appointments to be made, I tend to schedule them in the afternoon. My distance family, in the U.S.A. and the U.K., are asleep then and there's no chance of a missed call. You normally won't find me at the supermarket or hairdresser in the morning. Distance sons and daughters would likely laugh at the way I plan my day and maybe they are right, but while I have the luxury to do so, my response is 'why the heck not?' I want to make it easy for my family to connect. If they constantly find me in the car attending to errands it makes communication unnecessarily tricky, especially when little children are involved. I don't want them thinking twice before they pick up the phone.

Just a postscript thought to distance sons, daughters and grandchildren who are reading this. If you say you're going to ring at a certain time, your parents/grandparents will happily rearrange their worlds to be available. That might mean getting out of bed promptly even after a bad night's sleep or putting off a friend who suggested an outing. The odd slip up on your part or missed call will always be forgiven but please don't make it a habit. Quite honestly, Distance Parents and Distance Grandparents would rather stick with random potluck calls than pre-arranged calls that regularly fall over.

On the flip side, Distance Parents and Grandparents, *you* can't forget either. Leave a note, set the alarm and be sure your phone isn't accidentally on silent!

3. Quality versus quantity
Quality communication versus quantity of communication - is one better for you than the other?

Skype was the focus of Irish sociologist Rebecca Chiyoko King-O'Riain's research. She considered how this digital platform allows distance families to interact via continuous connectivity: keeping Skype turned on while life goes on around the device. A case of quantity over quality?

I have tried this communication option during a family meal gathering. However, when my distance family are dressed in pyjamas noisily eating cornflakes and we're enjoying an evening meal with a glass of wine, there is a sense of befuddlement. Of course, none of this matters, but given a choice I would prefer a shorter call, when the time is right, rather than a longer call in a muddly situation. King-O'Riain concluded that distance emotions of love and longing are lessened through this routine so it is a good solution for some.

The issue of quality versus quantity can transition as Distance Grandparents age. When we are younger and perhaps still working, connections might occur less often (quality, rather than quantity). However, when we age and are more housebound, then quantity, rather than quality, might become a greater priority. Frequent calls chatting about the everyday can be a welcome, regular distraction.

The question of quality versus quantity applies in both directions. As Barry (N.Z./England) grumbled, "I find phone calls sometimes difficult and often they are chatting while they are doing something else and not looking at each other [...] like sitting in a car going somewhere. Sometimes you get a better conversation when the setting is quiet and prearranged." Barry's distance family is understandably being time efficient by using their driving downtime to connect with home but the result is second best for the grandfather. A case of neither quality nor quantity.

There is no hard and fast rule about quality versus quantity but there is wisdom in knowing your needs may change and it's good to let the family know.

Beth (East Coast U.S.A./Zambia) highlights a less obvious by-product of distance family communication: "Thank goodness for WhatsApp! We talk with our granddaughter every day - singing songs, sharing books, playing with toys that are the same in each of our homes. They have a live-in nanny and I have been able to get to know her. I hope and pray our granddaughter will know us very well when we finally are able to get together! I actually get to have much more quality time with my granddaughter than many people I know whose children live in the U.S... It's just not in-person time."

4. Pretence: 'we're fine'

There are many reasons pretence exists between families. Do you hesitate to tell your distance family how you *really* are? There can be benefits in sometimes showing vulnerability.

There *is* a difference between casually saying 'how are *you?*' compared with a deliberate and slow... 'how *are* you?'

Here is an unsettling and brave reverse story of pretence. Dr Karen Eriksen is a distance daughter living in Sydney and recounts communications with her Distance Parents in Germany.

"Then came the internet with Skype, FaceTime and WhatsApp," Karen said. "Although advantageous in the sense that the elderly parents could now see the grandkids, son-in-law and dogs on the other side of the world, it was also very hard for my mother to get going with the technology, a struggle every Sunday night. Often, we gave up and just spoke on the phone. We never talked about feelings and worries, but both pretended everything was fine all the time, even when it wasn't, so as not to upset the other [...] My mother couldn't tell me on Skype how much worse my father's health was, as he could hear her, and I didn't want to worry her about my teenage son's depression in the hope she wouldn't find out ever. Just keep smiling!"

As a Distance Parent, pride can get in the way when things aren't good at home. Overwhelm can easily take over. You don't want to bother your family with your woes. The reality is this strategy isn't helpful for anyone.

In reverse it is hard when you *think* there is something wrong with your distance son, daughter or grandchild, but you aren't absolutely sure. In *Emotions and Relationships* I write of non-interference with the middle generation. Only you will know if it is right to prod and poke a little further.

When Karen reflected on her family dynamics, she wished she had added letter writing to their communication arsenal: "If we had written to each other [...] likely we would have poured our hearts out and given the other time to react to bad news."

My message here, once again, is there are no hard and fast rules. Look to adding *another* communication strategy or medium to your arsenal in the way Karen wished letter writing may have helped her mother. When you need to communicate on delicate matters you'll be relieved to have options. Don't have all your eggs in one communication routine basket.

5. Group versus one-on-one
Regularly connecting with distance family, as a *group*, offers fun dynamics, but as with the previous example there can be benefits in mixing things up.

In *Key Findings: The How It Is* I wrote of *Alone time - the greatest gift*. Group video calls are wonderful but dedicated, distance alone-time conversations are a gift and help you upgrade communication from light and fluffy to deep connections.

If you are one half of a grandparent couple and would prefer to occasionally talk one-on-one to a distance family member, this is understandable - and what's more, a good thing. It is sensible that either of you are able to connect in the case of an emergency and, likewise, neither is bothered by the other's actions. It's also a potential solution to Karen's problem above. If it was normal for her mother to phone by herself, the truth may have come out much earlier.

In reverse, are your distance grandchildren old enough to be responsible for connecting with you one-on-one, say once a month? If you would love to start a new routine like this gently raise the subject and plant a seed. You could even write your distance grandchild a chatty letter and add the suggestion in a relaxed *P.S.* This is a win-win for your distance family as it is sharing the task of connecting with family back home.

6. On stage

It's interesting to reflect that communication with distance family is dominated by video chat platforms while in-country family communication is likely by text, email or simply phone and, of course, visiting. Distance families are therefore continuously on stage - needing to perform. For some this is a burden.

> **❝ Distance families are continuously on stage - needing to perform. For some this is a burden. ❞**

There are people of *all* ages who honestly don't like video communication. They wish they weren't constantly being seen.

If you are among those who don't like being on camera, your options may seem limited. If you speak up, likely you will find some family members are very understanding, but others can't understand *why* you feel that way and could even be upset and see it as an affront. You could be opening a proverbial can of worms. The solution instead is to be the initiator of other *new* mediums of communication. For example, text for no reason, or write a letter for no reason.

In reverse, if you have family members who tend to be quiet during video calls then *they* could be the uncomfortable ones. Once again, mix things up. Send them a text or letter for no reason and see what happens. If they are uncomfortable with video calls you can be sure they'll respond with enthusiasm to other forms of communication.

The outcome of this strategy is that those who dislike video communication won't feel so obliged to be present during *every* future group video call because they have already chatted - albeit via a different method.

Pyjamas Don't Matter
Pyjamas Don't Matter is the apt title of a New Zealand child-

rearing book by David Geddis and Trish Gribben. Its theme is 'don't sweat the small stuff'. The same theme applies to Distance Grandparent communication.

Most times, if we are expecting a morning call, my husband and I try and be up, dressed and ready to go - on cue to happily perform. Likewise, at the other end of the day, if a call is anticipated, we'll resist a second glass of wine with dinner, knowing we'll be talking until late. Sometimes though, unexpected calls, especially in the mornings, can find us unwashed and still in our pyjamas with our hair at all angles. Distance Grandparents who aren't prepared to be flexible about appearances likely miss out. Ideally, concerns about keeping a degree of decorum and not being on stage in your dressing gown should be tossed to one side.

In contrast to these dynamics I rarely see my local, in-country family in their pyjamas or vice versa. In some respects when our distance family see us dressed this way they see a very human, down-to-earth side of us - and that's a good thing.

7. The written word

You will have gathered by now the written word is a valuable strategy in your Distance Grandparenting arsenal. We all don't write enough letters. As older people we remember how snail mail was part of the tapestry of life. When my husband was a young man, he had a summer job as a *postie* (mailman/postman). The New Zealand Post Office would recruit additional staff to cope with the huge volume of Christmas cards. Our children would likely have no memory of this. Our grandchildren rarely receive posted mail as most communication is electronic now. As grandparents we probably don't realise how special it is for our family to receive a handwritten note. You can be assured none of your old-fashioned efforts are tossed onto the kitchen counter and forgotten about. Instead, your letters are likely prized possessions, opened when the moment is right and filed away in a special place. When the postage for parcels is ridiculous, the cost of sending a card or letter is money well spent.

The day I wrote this topic I was coincidentally amazed and delighted to discover in my letterbox an old-fashioned, tartan-emblazoned postcard from my 21-year-old granddaughter who is on a working holiday in Edinburgh. She might be a digitally focused Gen Z-er, but she also treasures the written word. I read it, then re-read it, and for the rest of the day I felt special. She had taken the time to think of her Distance Grandparents.

"Receiving their very own letters with their names on the envelope makes grandchildren feel important, thereby building self-esteem."
Selma Wassermann, *The Long Distance Grandmother*

When I read Selma's words it was a timely reminder I hadn't put pen to paper for a while. I immediately stopped what I was doing, typed individual letters with photos and illustrations and put them in different coloured envelopes for my small American grandsons. A couple of weeks later my daughter video called and the envelopes were opened in a crazy, toddler-filled session of mayhem. Despite the pandemonium the boys absolutely knew who those letters were from.

"My dad sends cards regularly. You know what it is like in the States, every [public] holiday. He is always sending cards for Valentine's Day, Grandchildren's Day, birthdays and the likes. There is always this physical mail coming and it is his way of staying in touch."
Anna Seidel (American distance daughter in Germany)

"It is good to have nice letters coming through. They must be personal, one for Thomas and one for Nathan [grandkids in Switzerland]. Then they can say 'It is MY letter from Grandma,' not one for both of them."

Hannah (England/Switzerland and U.S.A.)

You have to keep working at being a Distance Grandparent and we all need a nudge here and there. Making a decision to occasionally write to each grandchild will always bear fruit.

Final Sage Advice

"If you want your children and grandchildren to reach out to you more often, be the most positive, encouraging, grace-filled parent and grandparent you can be. It's okay to be honest with your kids and grandkids from time to time, but don't make your own misery the main topic of conversation every time they call, or they will definitely stop calling. Instead, learn to forgive, focus on the positive, and enjoy your family every time you have the opportunity. Ask questions and focus on their feelings more than your own and you will definitely get a lot more calls [...]"

Wayne Rice, *Long-Distance Grandparenting*

The consensus among Distance Grandparents is information technology is a blessing in our lives. We remain grateful we are communicating from afar now and not a few decades ago.

EMOTIONS AND LOSS, ACCEPTANCE AND RESILIENCE

"Contemporary forms of global capitalism encourage an internationally mobile labor force. In order for this economic system to run smoothly, one might expect that people's emotional expectations - their emotional repertoire - would have to be in sync with the demands of mobility. In other words, a globally mobile labor force would seem to require emotional expectations that enable parents and children to live apart."

Cati Coe, *The Scattered Family*

Professor Coe from Rutgers University in New Jersey has written extensively regarding the geographical separation of families, with a focus on West African immigration to the United States. In her publication, with the apt title *The Scattered Family*, she makes the gutsy comment above. Coe's statement is a big ask.

Emotional Bricks and Mortar

Distance Grandparents' communication routines, as discussed in the previous chapter, are like the bricks of a solid wall. Bricks are tough, durable and full of purpose. Between the bricks is the mortar: a carefully calculated binding, weathering storms and hopefully lasting for generations. However, getting the binding just right is for most Distance Grandparents a continuous work in progress.

Distance Grandparenting emotions, good and bad, are ambiguous and unruly. They lurk around corners ready to spring unexpectedly upon us. When they find a porous gap they're sometimes difficult to shake free. Distance can have the effect of heightening some emotions and lessening others. Some emotions are short-term while some linger for years. Just as quickly, emotions can disappear under the radar and new ones appear as things change or the absence of daily encounters and the existence of voids offers little fuel for their continued presence.

Professor Zlatko Skrbiš, mentioned in *Unpacking Grandparenting and Distance Grandparenting*, advocates an awareness of the emotional complexities of distance family life. Concepts such as gender and class dominate social sciences and enjoy an elevated status in studies of transnationalism. He argues emotions deserve the *same* prominence. Interestingly, he states the discipline of Anthropology (my discipline) is less likely to neglect emotions and has a rich tradition of taking sentiments and emotions seriously, while other disciplines are not as proactive. I appreciate this opportunity to *tell it* as *it felt* in an honest, vulnerable way.

Emotional labour

Skrbiš also talks of 'emotional labour' that allows family relations to function across space and time. This involves the blending of traditions and family expectations with a sense of duty and obligation.

> *"There's emotional labor in being a grandparent because you need to pretend like you're happy because you are, but you're also sad at the same time, or overwhelmed, or needing space."*
> Sundae Schneider-Bean, *Expat Happy Hour*

I had no certainty as to how, when, where and why emotions would make themselves known when I began this project. I had many questions. I wondered whether Distance Grandparents would think and feel the same as me or react differently. Among my questions, were:

- Were grandmothers, overall, more proactive Distance Grandparents than grandfathers?
- Would some of my grandmother friends, who typically share lots of emotions with me when we are together one-on-one, present themselves a little differently when their husbands were present?
- Would I uncover grandparents who are unemotional about Distance Grandparenting and positively embrace their role?
- Would grandfathers show their vulnerable side?
- Are my own emotions about Distance Grandparenting just one version of how one can feel?
- Will there be tears, including my own?
- Should I carry extra tissues in my handbag when I visited my research Distance Grandparents and have a box nearby when I read my own and contributors' stories?

I can report that the answer to all these questions was a profound 'yes' and the reason is simple: globalisation and the process of migration disconnects families.

Absence and Presence

"[...] less presence doesn't equate to forgotten presence."
Dr Ray Guarendi, *Being a Grandparent*

Distance Grandparenting is not just about the *presence* (communication and visits); it is also about the *absence* (voids, silences, memories and empty spaces) and the opaque boundaries in between. A conundrum exists when you need to write about the meaning of that which is absent. A physically present grandparent connection with distance family *can* exist, but only periodically and involves air travel expense, which is an obstacle for some. Those moments of physical presence are savoured highlights but in between is, for most, an unsettling, longitudinal absence, with ever-present ambivalent emotions. The Welsh have a word for this - *hiraeth* - which means the longing, yearning or desire for a state that is, or was, no longer there.

Norwegian Professor Lars Frers writes in *The matter of absence* that the void is felt the most by those with the deepest ingrained attachment to that which is missing. Absence goes as far as invading the flesh provoking hurt, pain, fear and wonder. When an absence is felt, Frers explains, it has to be filled with that person's emotions to help bridge the emptiness. This explains why emotions are ever-present for Distance Grandparents.

I remember deciding to delay cleaning our glass sliding doors when my distance family returned home. I wanted to retain the knee-high, toddler fingerprints for just a bit longer. When I saw the fingerprints and sensed my grandson's imaginary presence, my feelings of absence and emptiness were both heightened and lessened.

"I feel, probably, I'm feeling the distance more than Ken [husband] is because I've had more time with our other [local] grandchildren than Ken has. I've done bedtime with them. They have stayed with us."

Nancy (N.Z./England)

"It is only four months since they left - but it seems like four years." (And later recounting a heart-wrenching question from her nearly four-year-old granddaughter) "Are you coming to England for my birthday?"

Rebecca (N.Z./England)

In a conversation with Karen (N.Z./England) she brought up Geoffrey Blainey's *Tyranny of Distance*: "There is a tyranny about the distance as you can't control it. You don't have the softening that a physical presence can provide so if you've got a family member who is struggling and you are watching it... it's agony for you to see. You are also seeing a filtered version. You see them in a crisis but you don't see them the next day when things might be better."

Absence and presence for Distance Grandparents are either all *on* or all *off* - there is rarely a middle of the road, in-betweenness. It can be both joy-filled, while exhausting, then hollow and lonely.

Answerphone message:
"Hi Helen. The kids have returned to London. I know I need to get your port-a-cot back to you, but I am not... ready to pack it up yet. The house is so empty. I will be in touch soon."

Lynley (N.Z./England)

An appreciation of the absences of Distance Grandparenting contributes to a deeper understanding of how Distance Grandparenting *is* and how those affected define, negotiate and understand themselves through these periods.

And... co-presence

In *Key Findings: The How It Is* I talked of the multi-sited places of Distance Grandparenting:

1. The grandparent's empty home
2. The grandparent's busy, full home during visits
3. The full distance son or daughter's home when visited by the Distance Grandparents
4. The virtual home of cyberspace

Numbers one to three are physical places of co-location, where people connect face-to-face. Even the grandparents' empty home, in a symbolic way, is a place of co-location as the home is likely filled with photos, birthday cards and gifts to be packaged. Sewing, knitting, wood craft and other projects may be sitting awaiting completion. A port-a-cot, highchair, car seat and other infant paraphernalia are stashed in a cupboard, basement or garage. Thoughts and conversations of downsizing the house may have occurred. The decision to retain a larger home, with the spare bedrooms, is for some a deliberate act of Distance Grandparenting.

The reality of Distance Grandparenting though, is the majority of the relationship is performed at no. 4 - in the cloud, as discussed in the previous chapter. Technology has created the digital concept of *virtual intimacy* where people mutually agree to make themselves accessible for contact. This is known as *co-presence*: the real-time places of video, phone calls and the like. In addition, continuously accessible online photo libraries, blogs and family members' social media platforms add another layer to the co-presence of distance familying.

> *"For transnational families, exchanging images has become a mode of maintaining familial bonds and facilitating a sense of co-presence across long distances."*
> Sinanan et al., *International Journal of Communication*

I am currently afforded a unique co-presence platform for which I am most grateful. My Chicago-based son Robbie is a radio presenter on a classical music station. At least once a week and thanks to live streaming, I am able to partake of my breakfast listening to his familiar Kiwi accent, knowing he is safely ensconced in the studio, working an afternoon shift. What's more, this co-presence can be shared. My mother, his grandmother, regularly tunes in too.

Decades ago when cyberspace never existed, the departure of a loved one to a far off land felt like a funeral. Few would argue with scholars who state that contemporary long-distance relationships are revitalised, strengthened and reaffirmed on a regular basis through this virtual, proxy, physical and imagined co-presence - they describe it as the 'de-demonising of distance' (Baldassar et al.).

The Senses

> *"[...] people's knowledge of themselves, others and the world they inhabit, is inextricably linked to and shaped by their senses."*
> Professor Andrew Sparkes, *Ethnography and the senses: challenges and possibilities*

The West most values the senses of sight and hearing (note, this is not the case in all cultures). Though the senses of sight and hearing via the use of information technology are somewhat satisfied for Distance Grandparents, the sense of touch and the yearn for even the briefest of cuddles remains starved.

Tiffany Field is a Development Psychologist based at the University of Miami School of Medicine and also the Director of the Touch Research Institute. She describes touch as a 'hunger' and highlights its healing qualities and the importance of touch for the elderly - the subjects of this book. Touch, she observes, is the mother of all senses.

She reminded me of a personal touch sensation experience that jolted my awareness of the senses and how they relate to the absences of Distance Grandparenting. Senses are complex and unpredictable and creep up on you when you least expect it, as my next story demonstrates.

One day, Susan, a young mum neighbour, called out to me as I was walking past her neat corner house. She invited me inside to have a cuddle with her newborn - her second son, Simon. Surrounded by toddler activity, toys, half-folded laundry and baby paraphernalia, I found a gap on the couch. I cradled the adorable six-week-old and from nowhere tears poured down my cheeks. I was somewhat embarrassed. *What's happening here?* I thought. After some quick summation I reassured my concerned hostess and toddler nothing was wrong. I realised it had been several months since I had visited my small grandchildren in America and when I cradled Simon the vacuum of my sense of touch was momentarily exposed in a raw and vulnerable way.

Professor Elisabeth Hsu from Oxford University also has a strong interest in sensory experiences and emphasises in her *Ethnos* article how one cannot overestimate the social and contextual nature of the senses. She notes how a particular social situation can elicit unique sensory experiences - they can be situation-specific, exactly as it was for my experience at my neighbour's home. The sensory order of any particular culture, or a family group like Distance Grandparents, must be understood on its own terms. Senses-filled stories are at the heart of Distance Grandparenting

At one stage Rhonda and Colin (N.Z./Germany) lived under the flight path close to Auckland Airport. Rhonda recounted, "I only had to hear the aeroplane coming over [when their son was expected] and I knew it was him... 'we've got to go... he'll take an hour to get through.'"

"One of the things I love about Georgia and Rose [distance granddaughters] being in England is we hear them speaking and they've got these beautiful accents and you can't believe they're a product of us. I think we miss out. We regularly see these little ones on FaceTime and technology has been an absolute godsend. We see them and they see us so we are not losing contact but we can't touch them or play with them. An annual week or two [visit] is probably not enough from my point of view."

Karen (N.Z./England)

"Little Odette looks pretty cute. It's difficult to see all these photos of her and not be able to touch and smell her!"

Gabrielle (N.Z./East Coast U.S.)

"I hope she will remember my voice."

Nancy (N.Z./England)

Visual contact was especially crucial to Maureen (N.Z./East Coast U.S.). She said, "I like to have quite a bit of facial contact so she can start to recognise us because I have been thinking too, if we are going back there in August to babysit and she doesn't know us very well that could be a tough assignment and I do not want a tough assignment."

Visits in either direction have our sense of smell working overtime. Houses have smells, neighbourhoods have smells and different weather has smells. At the most basic level there is adjusting to soiled nappies (diapers) and the fragrance of a different brand of washing powder and fabric softener. I have a travel-sized Johnson talcum powder in my sponge bag. I love to sprinkle some on my little grandsons as the perfume awakens memories for me of bathing my own children when they were infants. For me, it is a scent of love and caring.

Sundae Schneider-Bean regaled a story about a shrine in her mother's home in the States: "My mom has this little shrine - a collection of baby things and infant clothes. I remember a left-behind, stray sock in its unwashed state found a home in the shrine. The sock smells like her boys."

These examples demonstrate how stimulated senses connect the experience of parenting with the experience of grandparenting. Nostalgia, imagination and memory are all activated in the sensory moment of the present.

Australian-based Hendrika is a distance daughter from South Africa and co-author of *Your D.I.Y. Move Guide to Australia*. Her story confirms there is value in exchanging personal items with family members, so each party has in their possession a vault of human closeness: "My late dad was a pipe smoker. I have his tobacco tin which smells exactly like him. I open it from time to time when I truly miss him."

When family leave, there are lingering smells like leftover toiletries in the bathroom and the whiff of perfume on the bed linen, before it heads for a wash. In no time the inevitable clean-up occurs, the visitor smells dissipate and normality returns. Why is it when a stray kiddie sock appears one is automatically drawn to breathe in every thread?

Sensory experiences are complex and reveal neither a consistent pattern nor a set of norms. How do you make sense (excuse the pun) of Distance Grandparenting sensory experiences when some are experienced in an empty void, others in a virtual co-presence situation and some are showered upon oneself in chaotic, noisy in-person connections? The evidence again points to ambiguity and unruliness. We're wise to embrace this sensuous flux as an unsettling while still reassuring default setting of Distance Grandparenting.

Loss and Grief

Some losses are an inevitable part of life. The confronting possibility of children and grandchildren living thousands of miles away was never an inevitable loss and can therefore evoke grim, unsettled feelings and ongoing wavering expectations. As explained by Robyn Vogels and Hendrika Jooste in *Your D.I.Y. Move Guide to Australia*, migrants and expats close the chapter on an important part of their life when they move overseas and it affects more than just them.

The emotions of loss, grief and acceptance are hard to tidily differentiate. Yes, one generally follows the other, but not always.

When Rhonda (N.Z./Germany) spoke of her distance son's early travels from a couple of decades back, before he settled permanently overseas, she gently intimated to her husband, "We did miss him - didn't we?" Her husband replied tenderly, "We still do." Later Rhonda commented, "When Stuart [distance son] leaves, the tap [her tears] turns on."

"So in a way, I do miss the kind of day-to-day things [...] It is hard to imagine Lisa [granddaughter] growing up in London. It is such a big city."

Nancy (N.Z./England)

The following interview was my most emotional, though not my only one with tears. Each time I have read the transcription I am taken back to the moment and my eyes water.

Me: How is Distance Grandparenting for *you*?
Lynley (N.Z./England): I don't know why, but you suddenly make me want to cry... just thinking about it. [Out of our chairs for a hug.] I just... I just feel like I am totally missing out. I have never cried about this before. I am *it* [the *only* grandparent] and *I* am missing out.
Me: And the child is missing out?
Lynley: Yes, yes... I can't believe how much you have made me think about it [tears from both of us, another hug and off to the next room for tissues] and I guess, you know I never really... I have never minded Maria being away overseas... until this little one had come along and then I felt it... tug at your heart. There is another member of the family there... and just accept it and be pleased. That's the most important thing.

Whenever I bump into Lynley I remember and appreciate her honesty during this chat. She exposed her vulnerability and I exposed mine and felt her pain. As a single Distance Grandparent she has no one to bounce off her day. Furthermore,

I could appreciate the empty space of resilience she occupies as the *only* grandparent of her distance family package and the responsibility she feels it carries. Elisabeth Hsu explains people can communicate through simultaneously felt emotions, memories and sensations. My tears were a heartfelt simultaneous experience, and on many occasions during the writing of this book I have experienced watery eyes, laughed and cried, often while sitting alone at my desk.

Ambiguous loss

Emeritus Professor Pauline Boss, from the University of Minnesota, is known for her study of families, stress and loss. When I first came across her writing I was immediately at home. She understood how I felt as a Distance Grandparent and she delivered bountiful a-ha moments.

Boss is the principal theorist of the concept of 'ambiguous loss': a loss that always remains unclear. She first applied the theory in the 70s when studying families. Boss noticed physically present fathers were often psychologically absent, which resulted in an uncertain loss for their families. From these observations emerged the concept of ambiguous loss, representing the psychological absence with a physical presence (70s fathers) and/or the physical absence with a psychological presence (distance families).

Distance Grandparents understand ambiguous loss. They haven't lost their distance family: their family hasn't died. They have, however, lost *how* they imagined their family would function. They have lost a slice of their identity and the nature of their perceived grandparent, senior years. Their distance family is around in spirit (photos, mementoes and things) - but they are not here physically.

❝ They haven't lost their distance family: their family hasn't died. They have, however, lost *how* they imagined their family would function. ❞

Ambiguous loss encapsulates the emotions of absence, presence, loss, grieving, acceptance and their accompanying senses-filled experiences. Boss's Minnesota colleagues Catherine Solheim and Jaime Ballard, when commenting on the former's research, state that families able to maintain regular contact are likely to experience less ambiguous loss. The theory of ambiguous loss goes a long way to explaining the nebulous, hazy, murky nature of the uncertain losses experienced by distance families.

It could be argued that in time Distance Parents and Distance Grandparents, through their inevitable journey of acceptance, should just accept as a norm the permanence of the physical absence of their distance family and the accompanying ambiguous psychological presence. After 30 years in this space I will never get over it or see our family situation as normal. I do, however, *accept* it.

Acceptance – Two Steps Forward and One Step Back

The acceptance *of* Distance Grandparenting *by* Distance Grandparents is a finding intimated in all research similar to my own. It surfaces as a result of a loss, followed by a period of grieving and then a reluctant acceptance, to varying degrees, by Distance Grandparents of their scattered family package. I would describe it as layers of loss, grief and acceptance - woven over time.

Maureen (N.Z./East Coast U.S.) summed it up well: "I see acceptance as a grieving process. Sometimes, you take two steps forward and one back, but you are moving forward the whole time and as you are improving you're accepting that... you're understanding it. It is a loss. We have these ideals and these expectations that our children will marry and bring up their children in this land [New Zealand], with all the things we enjoy. It is a loss you have to accept and move on."

Anthropology and Sociology Professor Loretta Baldassar from Perth, Western Australia, has spent her career studying transnational caregiving and communication, working with immigrants in Perth and their family from afar. Alone, and in collaboration with colleagues, she writes extensively about caregiving in an international arena. A key collaboration is *Families Caring Across Borders* - a publication I'll regularly refer to. Her commentary is delivered with what I would call a degree of 'down-under' down-to-earthiness: a reflection of how Australians (and New Zealanders) tend to view life. She sums up that Australian distance families (and I would add New Zealand), in general, *do* adjust their worlds and live together across a distance.

This finding mirrors my thoughts on acceptance. I describe it like telling your kids they have to eat their veggies: "You don't have to *like* the veggies, you just have to *eat* them." You don't have to *like* the fact that you are a Distance Grandparent. You just have to *accept* it, because that's what your son or daughter passionately want you to do.

The 3 H's - the Language of Progressive Acceptance

The reluctant acceptance of Distance Grandparenting, without a high degree of complaint, is the norm for some but not for others.

Israeli scholars Laura Sigad and Rivka Eisikovits researched American Distance Grandparents and their relationship with their married daughters and grandchildren living in Israel. Frequently they reported the grandparent role as being compromised - 'taken away' - from their American grandparents.

I have met grandparents who can't accept *why* their child would ever want to live outside their own country and continuously ask *when* they are coming home. This is an extreme position and I would suggest is unhealthy for family relations.

Acceptance occurs in your heart. However, that doesn't mean Distance Grandparents don't sometimes moan and groan to a good friend - and that's fine. We're all human. When acceptance *hasn't* found a home yet, often its progress can be monitored by language. It's not so much about what you say to *yourself* (or your friends) - it's what you verbalise to your *distance family*.

This language is what I call *The 3 H's*: the Language of Progressive Acceptance.

One of the most heart-warming acceptance responses I've read was featured in an article by Dr Holly Sevier, a writer and teacher from Hawaii who interviewed local Indian grandparents with children in mainland U.S.A. One of the grandfathers explained, "I am constantly accepting whatever they are doing [...] that they are leading their lives, that they are doing well." Later he adds he feels he has changed as a result of this open-mindedness but also that this mindset has brought them closer, despite living a continent away. "They respect me tremendously [...] There's a tremendous relationship going on."

The 3 H's - Language of Progressive Acceptance of Distance Grandparenting

Level One - Harmful
"How dare you take my grandchild to the other side of the world. What is wrong with this country? Do we not have any say in your decision?"

A natural response, but likely destructive. Those words are never forgotten.

Level Two - Human
"I miss you so much. I can feel the distance. I just want to be there and give you all a hug. I wish you could come home."

Honest, understandable and still best shared with friends.

Level Three - Helpful
"This is *your* decision and I respect your choices. I am proud of you and will keep loving and supporting you from afar."

Wisdom that will reap benefits

Sevier acknowledged this grandfather was able to 'switch himself' to his children's way of thinking, remember the mindset of his own youth and give his family the freedom to grow and develop on their own. This is the most helpful level of Distance Grandparenting acceptance.

Remember, it's natural to occasionally revisit Levels One and Two. The crucial point is these thoughts aren't verbalised, at least to your distance family.

"You just have to adjust your thinking - and just accept it and be pleased - that's the most important thing."
Lynley (N.Z./England)

"When they left South Africa we missed them, but we did not pine after them as we wished them and their children well in their new environment."
Walter (South Africa/Australia and U.S.A.)

"Sadly, as much as you don't want to, you just have to accept they are not coming back."
Rebecca (N.Z./England)

"We were very lucky to be able to come to terms with having a global nomad for a daughter. We have learned to create a new way of life for ourselves and, although we miss having her and her family just round the corner, we have come to accept that perhaps they will never come home again."
Peter Gosling, *How To Be A Global Grandparent*

Once at a place of acceptance our minds do not buzz with resentful judgements. It's easier to be inventive about ways of connecting by thinking outside the box and, let's face it, it's better for our well-being not to resist *what is*. We have to take responsibility. We likely said to our children when they were young 'you can do anything' or 'dream big' or 'reach for the stars' and that's exactly what they've done. It just so happened their dream involved embracing a new place to live. They want us to be pleased for them and proud of their efforts.

Acceptance - being privy to the facts

A distance daughter pointed out to me that the middle generation share information with their Distance Parents based on the latter's level of Language of Acceptance. Right now, she is mentally preparing herself for another move, extending the distance between her and her Distance Mother by over nine hours. She knows her mother's language of acceptance sits at Level Two (human) and she hasn't broached the subject yet. "She will be devastated," she said. "If I knew she would respond at Level Three (helpful) she would be privy to much more information. My parents-in-law, however, have always supported us even though we knew they were sad about us not being closer. Our kids are their only grandchildren. I admire them and am grateful for their (Level Three) support."

The moral of the story is Distance Parents will feel ill-informed and out of the loop of what's going on if their level of Language of Acceptance adds yet another layer to the woes of their distance children.

Acceptance - the higher level

Kahlil Gibran in *The Prophet* writes, "Your children are not your children. They are the sons and daughters of Life's longing for itself. [...] You are the bows from which your children as living arrows are sent forth."

Solheim and Ballard went on to say that distance families, with similar physical barriers, may experience transnational loss in 'different ways'. Rosemary and Barry (N.Z./England) provided evidence of this. Their distance family package was similar to many grandparents I've met. I was startled to hear Rosemary and Barry emphatically *embrace* Distance Grandparenting and how they have adapted and thrived. I have spoken to many Distance Grandparents in my travels and none has given this response before. Our conversation deserves a special feature:

Barry: It's good for Rosemary because she can stop off [en route] in Singapore and visit family.
Rosemary: It works very well where they are in England and where I want to be. I like Distance Grandparenting.
Me: Why do you like it? (likely looking a little surprised)
Rosemary: I get the freedom of enjoying my own life without feeling that I need to keep... [pause]
Me: [...] every Saturday night free? [to babysit]
Rosemary: Yes, yes! (enthusiastically). I am free - totally free. No stress. That's what is important for me... no guilt.

Barry and Rosemary went on to share with me the many interests they have taken up in recent years, due to their freedom. Reflecting on my argument that Distance Grandparenting is the combination of many factors, I need to share their back story as it influences how Distance Grandparenting is for them.

Rosemary experienced a life-threatening health scare 10 or so years ago and thoughts of her health have made them reassess many things in life. She concluded, "I am trying now, in my old age - no regrets, no stress, to set them free. You have one couple here, who aren't upset about anything. I had twenty years [raising children]... then set them free."

For me, Rosemary and Barry are in a higher level, almost saintly, category of Distance Grandparents. They have coped with the fragility of a serious health scare and transitioned to a wholesome, uncomplaining acceptance of life. I admire their stance.

There is no one-size-fits-all response to Distance Grandparenting, which is symptomatic of modernity, individualism and globalisation. We're all different - and that's okay.

Envy

Envy as an emotion comes with a veil of negative connotations and doesn't sit in the same camp with loss and grief.

Dana Shavin in *Psychology Today* states that envy is not created equally. She cites Smith and Hee Kim who propose there are three types of envy: benign (wishing), emulative (desire to copy) and malicious (destructive). Distance Grandparents' envy is benign and, what's more, understandable.

Distance Grandparents need assurance it is normal to feel envious when a friend announces the birth of a local grandchild, or to quietly envy animated chatter over the fence of a neighbour's family gathering.

The following is an excerpt from a letter featured in Psychologist, Tanya Bryon's column in *The Times*. It is penned by Geoffrey, an English Distance Grandparent:

"We fully support his [distance son's] decision [to live in New Zealand] and we get on well with our daughter-in-law, but my wife and I still harbour some resentment towards them both. Although we know this is selfish and boils down to, 'Why have you done this to us?' and the feeling is not going away [...] We can find ourselves in tears when we see other grandparents with their grandchildren or even a man of about our son's age with a little boy."
Byron notes these emotions are normal and she congratulates

Geoffrey that he hasn't verbalised them to his down-under family. Envy is a natural emotion of Distance Grandparenting but the fact that it needs to be kept under wraps fuels my argument, Distance Grandparenting is a lonely place.

When Tanya Byron responded to Geoffrey she also said, "[...] without acceptance, mourning becomes a steady state and in time will have a negative impact on life and relationships."

Need to be Seen

Sundae Schneider-Bean raised a comment that piqued my curiosity. She said her mom always inquires as to whether Sundae's boys ask after her. Sundae's response to her mom is always 'yes'. She senses a desire from her mom to be noticed and not forgotten.

We all need to feel as if our presence matters to others - Toko-pa Turner in *Belonging* cites Henri Nouwen who says, "The simple experience of being valuable and important to someone else has a tremendous recreative power."

My personal experience is once a toddler grandchild has visited your home, or you have visited them, they never forget you. This is supported by psychologist Nancy Kalish, who writes in *Psychology Today*, "Lifelong attachments between grandparents and grandchildren can form even with relatively short periods of physical contact."

If you keep working at Distance Grandparenting the grandkids don't forget you, but they probably don't necessarily bring you up in conversations either - and that's just the way it is.

The Emotionally Resilient Distance Grandparent

This is a borrowed topic title, and not the first time I will refer to Linda Janssen's *The Emotionally Resilient Expat*. It is a classic read in mobility circles by distance sons and daughters. If the storyline of the subjects is reversed, the principles remain.

"Possessing emotional resilience doesn't mean we always remain upbeat or we don't suffer when bad things occur. What it does mean is we do our best to maintain or find our way back to a positive mindset - and view of ourselves - as quickly as possible. And by quickly, I mean as long as it takes."
Linda A. Janssen, *The Emotionally Resilient Expat*

A healthy level of emotional resilience as a Distance Grandparent is conducive to a smoother journey and is a by-product of achieving acceptance. There is no sense in getting offended when a distance toddler grandchild doesn't want to talk with Grandma on FaceTime. Similarly, if due to time zone issues your only chat times are their mornings and your teenage grandchildren continuously sleep in, it pays to go with the flow and not make a fuss.

Reserve your emotional resilience armour for the big things, because they will happen. When crises strike you'll be challenged... if you haven't already been. I have travelled this route and later you will read about times my emotional resilience headed disconcertingly close to empty; however, thankfully I bounced back each time.

I enjoyed what Australian Phil McAuliffe in *The Lonely Diplomat* had to say about bouncing back: "For resilience, the 'spring back' to regular status is critical. We revert to form - to our default behaviour and natural psychological state - once the event has passed."

The bottom line is our distance children have their hands full. Quite honestly, they have little capacity to cope with our troubles if we are feeling upset, forgotten about or offended. For them, living in a new country comes with a raft of daily challenges and, you're right, it's a situation *they* chose.

The Other Grandparents

In each distance family package, somewhere there is another set of grandparents or a grandparent - the in-laws of your distance son or daughter - who are hopefully still alive. They may live close or they may live far. They could be divorced, or with a new partner where the words 'step' and/or 'half' are part of the vocabulary. Perhaps they are of another culture or speak a different language. They may have welcomed your son or daughter into their family with a loving, caring embrace. Maybe they didn't - or at least that's how it feels.

> "The New Zealand grandchildren have a set of active N.Z. grandparents living nearby, and a large extended family there, so we feel they don't really need us."
>
> Anonymous (U.K./N.Z.)

If your distance son's or daughter's in-laws live handy there can be another reason for envy; however, it's best converted to gratefulness. Geographically close grandparents are mostly thankful for their good fortune and are very much aware of the distance the other grandparents cope with. The nature of each parental relationship is different and shouldn't be compared. Your distance son or daughter will tell you that.

EMOTIONS AND RELATIONSHIPS

> *"There are as many interpersonal problems in human relationships as there are waves in the ocean."*
> Selma Wassermann, *The Long Distance Grandmother*

Is there anything natural about being a grandparent who only gets to physically grandparent now and then? Scholars have claimed that globalisation makes the grandparents' role more ambiguous. I have talked about ambiguous loss - a *loss* that is unclear - and now I am talking about the ambiguity of relationships: *relationships* that are unclear.

Likewise, the concept of *ambivalence* within relationships will resonate with Distance Grandparents. Relationship ambivalence is experiencing both positive and negative feelings, or understandings of a situation, at the same time.

The quality of the grandparents' relationship with their distance children (and vice versa) is a barometer of how Distance Grandparenting *is*.

❝ The quality of the grandparents' relationship with their distance children (and vice versa) is a barometer of how Distance Grandparenting *is*. ❞

Even if the usual obstacles exist - like geographical distance, time zone inconveniences, expense of travel, inability or lack of desire to fly in either direction - a positive, warm relationship can exist if all parties are on the same page. However, ambiguity (unclear relationships) and ambivalence (mixed up feelings) will easily make themselves at home if any party of a distance family relationship isn't encouraging and supporting of their shared package. What's more, this also affects both directions of a grandparent/grandchild relationship.

Distance Parenting and Distance Grandparenting is not guaranteed plain sailing and I sense most take nothing for granted. They recognise regular recalibrating and re-orientating of relationships is necessary.

What happens when factors beyond grandparents' control affect the nature and harmony of their family package and geographical distance makes building and maintaining relations so challenging to navigate?

Gatekeepers and Gate Openers

I've noticed that the middle generation, our distance sons and daughters, are a powerful force and have the ability to make, break or muddy distance family relationships. Much of the time distance sons and daughters and their partners can be divided into two groups:

- *gate openers*
- *gatekeepers*

A gate is a pliable structure. Even if the hinges are rusty and loose and the gate tends to shudder as it drags across the ground, a bit of brute force and determination will open or close even the dodgiest of structures. Distance family relationships are the same.

Gate opener middle generation distance sons and daughters are proactive with communication and relationship building. They *enable* visits in either direction - even if they may have preferred a week at the beach by themselves. Gate openers know relationships are important and require constant attention. Super-achiever gate openers remember everyone's birthdays, even those of their partner's family. They set boundaries when they are required but do so from a place of caring. They do their best, most of the time, to make their distance family package work.

Gatekeeper middle generation children sit on the fence, are less than accommodating, mediate communication and/or can even be destructive of connections and relationship building. Visits in either direction are barely tolerated or perhaps even discouraged. Gatekeepers can be difficult and block alone time opportunities, as discussed in previous chapters. In other words, they make distance familying constantly difficult.

Thankfully, the majority of Distance Grandparents enthusiastically indicated that their middle generation are gate openers.

> "Whenever we go, she [daughter-in-law] makes us feel very welcome. She keeps saying over and over again: 'You are always welcome here. Don't ever feel you are imposing, because you are not.'"
>
> Maureen (N.Z./East Coast U.S.)

> "I have got a very, very happy family group. I am extremely fortunate, and I know that. They might not live where I would like to see them, they might not have what I want... but they have just this wonderful, happy bubble going on."
> Lynley (N.Z./England)

> "She [distance daughter] is a gate opener - definitely and she is the one who drives FaceTime. She is very regular."
> Karen (N.Z./England)

I came across examples where distance sons or daughters are less than supportive. The negative tendencies of gatekeepers don't come from nowhere. They can be triggered by a myriad of factors including strained marriages, prior breakdowns in communication, addictions, insecurities, a need for control and emotional baggage. Gatekeeper middle generation children rarely wipe the distance relationship, taking it to a point of estrangement, but they can do a jolly good job at bringing the relationship to a point where the Distance Grandparents wonder why they bother.

Shona and Brian (N.Z./Scotland) whose distance son is divorced and lives apart from his children and ex-wife were less than enthusiastic when we chatted. Theirs is a gatekeeper scenario and Distance Grandparenting comes with a lot of heartache. Below is our conversation...

Shona: We love all our grandchildren. We have the two in Auckland and know them inside out, back to front and love them to bits. Obviously, we love the ones in Scotland as well but that's been tenuous because the communications have always been [initiated] on our side and they are 12,000 miles away. So, we always instigate the phone calls on their birthdays and Christmas and we send them presents. We've seen them probably four times in the U.K. They have lived there about 10-12 years now. In 11 years, we have been there four times, so we don't know the ins and outs of them. Isobel [oldest distance granddaughter] has been pretty good at keeping in touch, especially as an adult. She will send us little messages or videos of what she or her brothers are doing... and that's nice. At the age of 16 she spoke to us and I'll never forget it. She said, "Omar and Opa, you have never forgotten our birthdays and even though things are up and down with our parents, that is special to us." We thought, *well if we can't communicate at least they know us and we are in their lives.* When Isobel gets married, it would be fabulous to go to the wedding.

Brian: If we're invited!

Shona: I am sure Isobel would invite us (laughing with hesitation, knowing nothing is a given).

As a postscript to Brian and Shona's story, when their distance grandchildren later spent two days with them during a New Zealand Christmas visit, an encouraging deeper connection was made and the feelings of grandparenting isolation and loneliness dissipated, albeit briefly. A year later, when I was visiting, one of these distance grandsons was in the country again and due to visit the following week. Out of the blue, a few days before he was expected, he texted to say he would be driving through their town, en route to his next destination and would pop in for lunch. There was a bevy of excited activity as lunch was prepared and urgent tasks attended to. Clive and I exited so when the doorbell rang they could give him their undivided attention. Despite the strained relationships progress was being made.

Just to divert a little, this couple's situation is additionally important as it shows evidence of one of my *Key Findings: The How It is* - that in-country family contribute to how Distance Grandparenting *is*. Brian and Shona's New Zealand daughter, son-in-law and two grandsons are very close and supportive and also grapple with the same distance family ambivalence and ambiguity. Brian and Shona tolerate and warily accept their distance family package as it is offset, to a generous degree, by the proactive love from their in-country family who you could say step up and unconsciously lessen the void. Distance Grandparenting for Brian and Shona is like a package deal; like a set of emotional scales they try and keep balanced, as best as they can.

Jim and Rebecca (N.Z./England) offer another gatekeeper scenario. As previously mentioned, they have a very close relationship with one distance granddaughter, son and daughter-in-law. I was aware Jim had other overseas children and grandchildren from his first marriage - a subject rarely mentioned. When I gently raised the topic of the other ones, I sensed emotions remained raw. Relationships with this other middle generation were strained (elements of gatekeeping existed). The result was their grandparent love was focused entirely on their one distance granddaughter, where communication was easy and the middle generation were *gate openers*. As described by Jim: "I have to be honest. I have never felt for anything, anybody, anything what I have felt for this little girl."

In another case I'd emailed Louise, a single Distance Grandmother, asking her to participate in my research. I later learnt why she hadn't responded. One day we shared a car returning from a mutual friend's funeral and emotions for all of us were raw. She lamented about her estranged son in New Zealand and I realised this was the father of her distance grandchild in Japan.

She reflected, "I should have responded to your email, Helen - but it [Distance Grandparenting] is hard."

Loss of mastery

Southern Californian scholars Linda Drew and Merril Silverstein discuss the well-being of grandparents in a *Journal of Family Psychology* article. A loss of contact with grandchildren as a result of divorce, family breakdown and gatekeeper tendencies is defined by the researchers as a loss of 'mastery', or the loss of control of your life. Grandparents like Shona, Brian, Jim, Rebecca and Louise have limited mastery of the relationships with their distance family.

Disaffected family may be disaffected whether they are local or distant and thoughts of them lurk in the minds of the grandparents. Shona (N.Z./Scotland) described it as 'eating away' at her. These stories contribute to the finding of loneliness: places of silent, helpless sadness... of trying to make sense of their family package. In all other aspects of life these grandparents function well, despite their distance burden. They learn to cope, to achieve a level of emotional equilibrium - at least on the outside.

I sense for these grandparents the shine and sparkle has been rubbed off a significant portion of their personal happiness and grandparenting experience.

Two sides to every story

After the last topic I need to insert a disclaimer. There *are* two sides to every story. I am sure there are distance sons, daughters, or their partners screaming at the previous pages saying, 'You haven't met my mother-in-law!' In support of this, Selma

Wassermann was rightly critical of grandparents who struggle to be open and non-defensive in their relationships with their distance family. She boldly states, "This may be difficult for many of us who have learnt to hide our vulnerability behind a façade of protective defensiveness. When we are confronted with unpleasantness, with anger, with hostility, it is much easier to try to defend ourselves against the assault."

I appreciate there *are* destructive Distance Parents and Grandparents who have made life very difficult for all concerned. Maybe this book will help. As I acknowledge my dilemma bear in mind this is the first of a three-book series. It tells *one* generation's side of the distance family story. I promise contributors to *Being a Distance Son or Daughter - a Book for ALL Generations* and *Being a Distance Grandchild - a Book for ALL Generations* will set the record straight in chapters on parent and grandparent gatekeeper tendencies. As the saying goes, 'Be sure to tune in next time'.

Mothers and Daughters, Mothers-in-law and Daughters-in-law

Do mothers have stronger relationships with their daughters and their offspring than they do with their sons and their children? All evidence suggests they do, and later many stories will be shared of grandmothers being there at important moments, like the time of the birth of a distance grandchild. Maternal Distance Grandmothers certainly accrue the most frequent flyer miles.

Paternal Distance Mothers are unfortunately burdened with the mother-in-law title: a title generating no end of nervous tension. Let me inject a little humour. Alexander McCall Smith is a prolific author. In one of his popular series he has these delightful words to say about mothers-in-law: "[...] you did not just marry a man, you married his father and grandfather, his grandmother and, most importantly, you married his mother. The last relationship was weightier than any of the others, because a mother-in-law could make or break a marriage, sometimes even without saying anything at all. Sometimes body language was sufficient."

Being a mother-in-law is never plain sailing and, once again, adding distance to the package means treading carefully. I sense a respectful overlay of caution by all mother-in-law Distance Grandmothers trying not to put themselves forward. My take on this family dynamic is mothers-in-law desire and cherish a warm relationship with their distance daughter-in-law but remain cautious, especially if the maternal mother is geographically close to her daughter. It's almost as if it is bred into us, that maternal relationships take priority over the paternal.

"There are nuances of being a grandmother and a grandmother-in-law. I do think it is different when it is your daughter who has had the grandchildren. You have a lot more license as a grandmother. When it is your daughter-in-law you don't have that. A friend of mine has a saying [about being the mother of the groom] to wear beige and say nothing... say nothing until you are asked. Talking [complaining] to the son causes a lot of problems, lots of dynamics. Who knew grandparents had to be diplomats as well?"

Karen (N.Z./England)

Karen is right; however, there are still exceptions to the rule. Two of my research grandparent couples have three sons each and no daughters and providentially both distance sons are better communicators than their in-country boys. Likewise, both distance daughters-in-law are totally supportive and in a small way are like the daughters they never had. I recall being relayed a story that also breaks with tradition, of a mother-in-law from Perth, Australia, who moved for a few months to West Coast U.S.A. to nurse her gravely ill daughter-in-law.

"The long and short of it is that every family is different and every set of relationships is different."
Gransnet, *The New Granny's Survival Guide*

Like mothers-in-law, daughters-in-law also attract bad press. I have met Distance Grandparents who report having what they describe as 'daughter-in-law from hell' family dynamics. These are my observations:

- These daughters-in-law have a need for control and display signs of insecurities as mentioned in *Gatekeepers and Gate openers*.
- The mother-in-law and/or parents-in-law can be a threat to the daughter-in-law's sense of stability.
- Even when the distance sons observe family dynamics that are unconducive to warm family relationships, they rarely speak up.

I will share a left-field, albeit extreme, distance daughter-in-law-from-hell story that will provide a glimpse to the worst of family upset.

Ken (N.Z./England) alerted me to a play being staged in Auckland. For decades, recently knighted playwright Sir Roger

Hall has humorously depicted older Pākehā (European) Kiwis as they are, warts and all, with tales of travel, retirement and old age. His latest two-person play, *Winding Up*, featured a retired New Zealand Distance Grandparent couple who had never met their two young grandsons who live in London. Their London *gatekeeper* daughter-in-law was as bad as they come and when I attended the production I was conscious of loud gasps from the audience. The first gasp occurred when the daughter-in-law made it blatantly clear, during an international phone call, her parents-in-law were *not* welcome to stay with them on an upcoming visit and more than likely the London family would not even be in town. The aftermath of the trip was the grandparents only saw their middle generation son and were never introduced to the boys: another audience gasp.

Ken knows Roger Hall through academic circles and in a later email he relayed, "Roger always does extensive informal research among friends before developing his scripts, so I assume the Julia [distance daughter-in-law] situation is based on a real case."

There seems to be so little the Distance Grandparents can do other than learn to tolerate the situation. I put this down to three reasons:

- Over time the son tends to sway towards the thinking of his wife: a case of *anything for peace or happy wife, happy life.*
- If their son isn't speaking up for his Distance Parents, the parent's hands are somewhat tied.
- Speaking up by the Distance Parents is likely to cause additional friction within the son's marriage and most parents feel this is a no-go territory. It could also lead to a lessening of opportunities to connect with the distance grandchildren.

In *Final Big-Picture Questions* there is discussion regarding addressing conflict.

Grandparent/Grandchild Relationships: Think of a Crockpot/Slow Cooker

This is a topic that troubles Distance Grandparents. They want to build bonds. They want to be close to *all* their grandchildren but there are obstacles between *some*.

> "When the grandchildren were very young, between birth and two years, I was this strange woman who appeared for two weeks a year."
>
> Kathryn (Zambia, U.K. and Egypt) cited in Gosling and Huscroft's *How To Be A Global Grandparent*

Kathryn's experiences are normal. Sometimes, in the early years, you wonder if you are making any impact with your video calls, parcels in the mail and visits. Please be assured seeds *are* being sown. Little things stick with children and later they remember and utter a random comment about something that happened years ago... and it blows you away. The last time my six-year-old grandson visited my home he was under two. However, he will still occasionally say "I remember your house" and describe a feature or two.

A couple of factors definitely help to build Distance Grandparent/ grandchild bonds and relationships:

- Was the grandchild born in the same country as the Distance Grandparents and remembers your home and having you around... or was the grandchild born overseas with little understanding or connection to home?

- Does your distance son or daughter (and partner) encourage and initiate all variety of connections with you? Are they intentional about this task? Do they speak well of you within the confines of their home... or do you have a *gatekeeper* scenario?

Both these factors matter and affect the level of bonding that can be achieved between grandparents and their distance grandchildren.

On our last visit to the States, our then four-year-old grandson was given an opportunity to stay with us in our next-door Airbnb. He was used to sleeping in different homes as his Mum and Dad co-parent. We chatted about this adventure and he was all for it. However, when it came time for lights out, a little voice whispered he wanted to go home. He knew us, we weren't strangers, but this was all too foreign for him. We weren't upset. We got it. Maybe next time?

My message here is Distance Grandparents need to accept, earlier rather than later, they will rarely have the same type of connection with their distance grandchildren as they have with those who are in-country, who sleep over and know every nook and cranny of your house. However, what you *do* develop with the overseas grandkids will brim with unique experiences and memories and still mean a lot to your grandchildren.

One other Grandparent/grandchild relationship factor must not be overlooked when we focus on the big deal topics like globalisation, mobility and distance familying:

Kids are kids! Grandchildren the world over do not turn out the same. Some are drawn to developing a close relationship with their grandparents, while others are more matter-of-fact about it all. It is no reflection on their upbringing, or *you*. Some children are inspired to keep in touch with Nana and Grandad, while others are not. Likewise, children go through phases of who and what are important to them. Some will experience a closer connection to your home country, others will always consider it a distant place. Distance Grandparents, who have more than one grandchild overseas, will likely already notice a closeness, for *no particular reason* with some, not all grandkids... and that's okay.

In conclusion, Grandparent/grandchild relationships take time to develop just like a casserole in a crockpot. Never give up, never feel what you are doing is a waste of time – just be patient that *it is what it is* and make the most of what you have.

Non-negotiable Relationship Factors

I remember learning as a child that the letters of the word 'assume' remind us of its meaning: to assume is to make an *ass* out of *u* and *me*. Parents may assume their distance son or daughter will retain the traditions of home and their heritage; however, time and new unions expose the middle generation to other ways of thinking.

The following non-negotiable relationship factors demand of the Distance Grandparents respect, tolerance and give and take. A degree of standing back and acceptance is needed if decisions made by your distance family don't sit perfectly with you.

Culture, religion and language

Culture, religion and a common language are like invisible threads binding a garment, and similarly bind distance families.

The odd stray thread here and there won't matter. However, when by necessity or choice distance family generations need to work within contrasting parameters, connections can weaken and cause the garment to fray. Distance Grandparents can purposefully or unwittingly contribute to this untangling.

They also have the option to navigate a way forward that avoids families unravelling, while graciously embracing the new and perhaps the foreign. The choice is theirs. As Csaba Toth, a global leadership coach, writes in her article 'Uncommon Sense in Unusual Times', "Culture is not who we are, it's what we're used to."

Distance Grandparents can become confused and disappointed, for example, if their native language isn't the first language of their grandchildren. Likewise, if somewhat strange (to them) religious holidays are celebrated overseas, bearing no relevance as they see it to the values and traditions of home, Distance Grandparents can get upset. If a new or additional religion has been embraced by their distance family, strong emotions can surface for the Distance Grandparents. These are predictable reactions. However, Distance Grandparents need to realise there is no flexibility; the decisions made are not ours to make and are non-negotiable.

Mariam Navaid Ottimofiore's robust publication, *This Messy Mobile Life,* provides a one-stop shop for all things multicultural, multilingual and multi-mobile, from the perspective of the distance son or daughter. The title confirms that the topics are complex and Mariam celebrates this diversity. She packs a punch when saying it is easier for some distance sons and daughters, with more complex families, to explain the nuances of their family to strangers, than it is to their own family and friends. This must be a burden to navigate.

Similarly, authors Erin Meyer in *The Culture Map* and David Thomas and Kerr Inkson in *Cultural Intelligence* delve into culture in the global workplace where people of starkly different backgrounds are expected to work harmoniously together. The authors encourage their readers to put to one side one's own culturally based assumptions and in a mindful and creative way apply certain techniques in cross-cultural situations. This is wise advice and applies to families too.

Peggy Fisher (East Coast U.S.A./Germany), now a Distance Grandmother and previously a distance daughter, was aware of this. She described when her young daughters travelled from Germany to Oregon, U.S.A., to stay with their grandparents they would sit in the back of the car and speak German to each other. That must have been a curious experience for Peggy's parents on the rural roads of Oregon.

A partial solution to bridging the language gap is for the Distance Grandparents to try and learn a few words or phrases. Grandchildren might enjoy being part of this learning experience and teach a few words online. Small efforts here demonstrate a willingness on the part of the grandparents to embrace their new family dynamics.

And what about when your distance family start to lose their accent and sound like the locals? My stepson, Guy, in no time acquired an upper middle-class English accent even though the locals likely say he still sounds very Kiwi. Lately I have noticed that my Georgia-based (U.S.A.) daughter utters plenty of 'y'alls' as her Kiwi accent melds with an emerging Southern drawl.

Differences never stop appearing. Distance Grandparents have a duty to work at empathising and accepting the cultural choices and changes of their distance middle generation. This is one of the greatest gifts we can give them. Will it always sit right? No. Is it what you want? Not necessarily - but that's not the point.

Respect

There is a mantra in our family I tend to spout forth on a regular basis. It wouldn't surprise me if it gets dragged out at my funeral eulogy or ends up on my gravestone: "It's not what you say... it is how you say it."

Jim Burns agrees in his delightfully titled book, *Doing Life With Your Adult Children: Keep Your Mouth Shut and the Welcome Mat Out*: "A conversation conveys respect; a lecture doesn't. [...] One of the greatest gifts you can give your children is to respect them as adults. If you don't give them respect, it's pretty much guaranteed they will close the door on your guidance."

... and Selma shares similar thoughts below.

"Respect is missing when grandparents are frequently critical; when they give unasked for advice; when they believe they know better what is right for the family and often say so; when they show little regard for the feelings and ideas of their children and grandchildren [...] Solid relationships are built on a foundation of respect."
Selma Wassermann, *The Long Distance Grandmother*

To a certain degree, Distance Grandparents have to be more sensitive than geographically-close family regarding zipping up and observing a respectful stance, because distance connections will usually be more fragile. In contrast, physically-close, in-country relationships have time and space to become robust. I can vouch for the fact it is easier to address tricky subjects with local family because it is simpler to navigate the best time and place to raise the subject and they can see the whites of my eyes.

Karen (N.Z./England) offered an insightful observation about navigating relationships: "I think there's a little bit of 'distance lends enchantment' to the view in that you know because... because you don't see them day-to-day. You don't see the things that drive your child crazy [about us] because in a phone call or a visit, unless you are there for months at a time, you are not going to see. And let's face it I think we can all live and sleep more comfortably if we think that's the case [preferred reality]. We tell ourselves that's the case... So much easier."

I love the sign Jim Burns describes that hangs in his office: "Every child needs at least one significant adult who is irrationally positive about them."

Non-interference: Put a Hold on Advice

The subject of non-interference is regularly raised by Distance Grandparents who don't want to be seen to offer unsolicited advice to their middle generation, but this isn't necessarily easy. This is a hot topic and the reason is two-fold:

- You never stop being a parent. Well-meaning advice can flow freely, without a moment's thought.
- Non-interference is herculean to enact. It takes a determined effort *not* to add your tuppence worth.

Let's face it, nobody, including our children, likes to be told they are wrong or there is a better way to do something.

"I've always tried to maintain... my children might beg to differ! I only give advice if they ask for it. It is hard because you can see stuff that is fairly obvious. But I think in time you gain respect and eventually they might say, 'What do you think?' It is music to my ears."

Karen (N.Z./England)

Jim Burns offers further advice when he says, "Words don't always lead to connection, but enjoyable connections lead to words." He sympathises because withholding advice goes against our nature as parents, but unsolicited advice he explains is *usually* taken as criticism. This is further complicated because some adult children can't distinguish between what we consider an innocent remark or desire to fix a problem, and parental control. He reminds his readers it is necessary to trust life experience is a better teacher to our children than parental advice.

> **❝ He reminds his readers it is necessary to trust life experience is a better teacher to our children than parental advice. ❞**

Even the most easy-going and content of grandparents have their moments of despair. I remember chatting with Lynley (N.Z./England) who has had 20-plus years' experience selling new-build houses and helping customers fine-tune their plans to get things just right. She described an overseas visit when her son-in-law, who was replacing the kitchen cabinets, made it clear her opinion and advice were not needed. We laughed and shrugged our shoulders.

The subject of non-interference is never far away for Distance Grandparents.

EMOTIONS AND BEING THERE

"Caregiving comes as close as anything I have encountered to offering an existential definition of what it means to be human."
Arthur Kleinman, *The Ground Between*

This chapter on emotions delivers the action behind the sentiments.

Arthur Kleinman lives in New York City. He is a Psychiatrist, Psychiatric Anthropologist and Professor of Medical Anthropology and Cross-cultural Psychiatry at Harvard University. Despite all his decades of learning it wasn't until his wife was diagnosed with a terminal illness and he chose to nurse her at home he understood, for the first time, what it meant to care. It profoundly affected him.

Being there, wishing to care for family, is an inbuilt desire, while simultaneously a pressure, instinct and obligation. For a traditional local grandparent, being there may take the form of a myriad of tasks and joys, including childminding, reading stories, arts and crafts, baking or practical driving and collecting from daycare and school. Distance Grandparenting from afar is a world apart.

Ghassan Hage is a Lebanese-Australian Professor of Anthropology at the University of Melbourne. He writes of French

Sociologist, Anthropologist and Philosopher Pierre Bourdieu's *illusio* (desire) and *habitus* (socially ingrained habits), "[...] to be simply deprived of purpose and orientation is to be deprived of raisons d'être, to be deprived of being." Distance Grandparents possess Bourdieu's *illusio* and *habitus* but cannot fully enact the role. They are denied the generally instinctive and heartfelt opportunity to care, to be there for their children and grandchildren, in a hands-on, day-to-day, practical way.

Professor Loretta Baldassar and colleagues (introduced in *Emotions and Loss, Acceptance and Resilience*) state in *Families Caring Across Borders* how long-distance caregiving, even with the geographical separation, binds intergenerational families. Love and trust fuel this co-operation.

> "Whether it is grandchildren or children, being available at the end of the telephone, is very important."
>
> Colin (N.Z./Germany)

> "Just being there. The growth is at that time and you experience it with him and if you are not there, he'll still grow but it's just, for my own sake [...] It's real - it is more real."
>
> Rosemary (N.Z./England)

Baby Bumps

Baldassar et al. maintain that once children arrive for the distance family, bonds are strengthened with their parents. However, the transition is not necessarily one of charming new-baby bliss.

The announcement

First-time grandparents (distance or otherwise) aren't all immediately captivated by their impending role, and experience an emotional tug of war. They may feel too young, or view grandparenthood as an old person's Rite of Passage they have no desire to experience... just yet. I can remember, albeit briefly, when my own daughter announced she was pregnant. I wasn't ready even though I had been a stepgrandmother for over 15 years!

Parents might be conscious they feel nothing maternal (or paternal) when they observe their grandparent friends interacting with their own grandchildren. There is no yearning to hug the little one and the grandparents-in-waiting can actually consider there is perhaps something wrong with them. *Shouldn't I want to hug this little one?* Considering all these things, for some Distance Grandparents-in-waiting, geographical distance can be a welcomed obstacle while they adjust their thinking.

For other parents, though, their first reaction to the pregnancy announcement is a loud cry of 'at last'. They are eager and ready for the impending arrival and new title. They can't wait to get on a plane and in some cases can be overwhelming in their desire to be there: a potentially frightening place for a hormone-filled, newly pregnant daughter-in-law, or even daughter.

However, for everyone, including the pregnant couple, the announcement is a rude awakening and a reminder of the geographical distance - and all it now means.

> "My son and daughter-in-law are moving to Amsterdam from Melbourne and she is pregnant with my first grandchild. Melbourne felt a bit doable, but this feels hopeless."
> Julie (N.Z./Australia)

"'Mother I'm pregnant,' came the message. It would not have caused much of an upheaval if the impending arrival was to be a few miles down the road, but there was no way that there could be rapid to-ing and fro-ing and watching the bump getting bigger gave us much food for thought. There was nothing that we could do, we felt very much left out."
Peter Gosling, *How to be a Global Grandparent*

Distance Grandparents all agree on two things:

1. Travelling to visit family with a newborn is a wait-to-be-asked scenario.
2. The middle generation do not want advice, as mentioned in the previous chapter.

Endless questions

The impending birth of a grandchild generates endless questions for the grandparents-to-be, including:

- Should I travel over?
- Will my daughter/daughter-in-law want me there?
- Should I try and be there for the birth, or travel later?
- How do I decide what dates to book my flights?
- What happens if baby arrives early, or late?
- Can I manage babysitting the toddler when the parents go to the hospital?
- [For grandparent couples] Should we both go, or just the grandmother?

Then there is the perennial question: *What will I be called?* Even a simple issue like this can cause a state of mild flux and

I remember experiencing that. *Nana* had already been taken by my own mother and I definitely didn't want to be Grandma or Granny. In the end my grandson decided for me when he uttered the mixed up title 'Nanma' and it has stuck ever since.

Once we have broken through all these psychological and emotional barriers, when the time comes every version of Distance Grandparent will do a 360-degree flip and be hungry for the tiniest morsel of baby news from afar.

American Dr Pat Hanson, who I will speak of in more detail in the next chapter, was a hesitant grandmother and recounts her feelings of meeting her first grandchild: "Then something in his five-month-old smile, his soft skin or the baby smells broke through my reluctance and made me admit I truly was a grandmother. More tears. When the heart opens they flow."

Similarly, Yvonne Quahe (East Coast U.S.A./England and Switzerland), an expat Human Resources and Global Mobility Professional, experienced the same response. She was also reticent about her new familial role. But as she explained, the first time she met this newborn bundle he made her feel *different*. She is surprised at how much she enjoys being with her grandson.

In time we need to tread cautiously as we enthusiastically share news of our new addition. A little restraint is in order, so as not to bore our friends. Selma Wassermann describes it as belonging to a 'grandparent fraternity': those on the outside do not understand what all the fuss is about. "You have to be a grandparent to know."

Unspoken questions

Despite the celebrations, in the back of the minds of Distance Grandparents and unlikely to be verbalised, are questions like:

- What relationship will I have with the grandchild?
- Will there be anything Kiwi/American/Canadian/English/ Australian/South African about him or her?
- Will they ever live where I live?

South African Distance Grandparents Walter and Sandra (U.S.A. and Australia) have done a lot of accepting. "Both grandchildren were born in the U.S.A. [...] they are developing as true Americans and we respect that and do not want them to change that," said Walter.

Baby support

In 1986, when the Distance Grandmothers featured in this book were busy mothers, Martine Segalen wrote *Historical Anthropology of the Family.* She writes of the distinctions of roles between spouses, high levels of contact with local parents and the importance of the relationship between mothers and daughters. This was the case for me during the 80s when I stopped working to have children and my mother was 10 minutes away.

Fast-forward and distance is no deterrent to Distance Mothers to be there if they can. Many Distance Grandmothers have flown independently, at least once, to be with their daughter. The grandfathers frequently said 'I would just be in the way' and 'I would be useless in that situation'. These comments could also be interpreted as a message to their wife to 'do what is instinctive'.

Rosemary and Barry (N.Z./England), with a new distance grandchild, spoke at length about their supportive role as grandparents (and parents). Offering practical support was, as far as they were concerned, a non-negotiable obligation they took extremely seriously. Parents can feel particularly compelled to visit after the birth of a grandchild if they sense the mother is struggling, which was the case.

Barry: The major concern has been Sally [distance daughter] hasn't been getting enough sleep and that's why Rosemary went [the first time]. It's imperative we keep Sally in good health.
Rosemary: That is the role of the grandparents who have had experience as being mothers and how, first-time round, sort of not knowing anything. I didn't have Mr Google, while she goes to Mr Google every time. Mr Google is not God. So, I think being able to help... this gives support. All grandparents need to. Whether their advice or support is appreciated or even taken in. It is not for us to deny them what... (hesitating)
Barry: [...] She has been asking for help. We were concerned about, you know, if she gets into some sort of depressive situation, which would be no good for either her, or the baby, so better to invest time.

Shortly after this chat, Rosemary flew alone to England for the second time to support her daughter, son-in-law and grandson. To enable this trip, the grandparents cancelled a previously planned overseas pilgrimage journey as it clashed with the England visit, a sacrifice they were happy to make. When I caught up upon her return, Rosemary recounted that she took on the nightshift duty while visiting and this enabled her daughter and son-in-law to enjoy more sleep and transition to a new stage of parenting. The baby (eight months) was now sleeping in his own room and the mother had been weaned off the baby monitor. Rosemary, who is a loving, but no-nonsense kind of woman, explained in a chuckling, caring manner she had not travelled halfway around the world for no reason. She had a purpose and had achieved the desired results.

A few years ago, a local Distance Grandmother friend related a similar story about visiting Europe at the time of the birth of her first grandchild. The new mother, her daughter, preferred her baby be unrestricted by blankets during sleep time. However, after some sleepless nights and finding the new mother in tears in the middle of the night, my friend reluctantly took over, swaddling the baby in a soft blanket. In no time bubs was settled, feeling securely enveloped in what some might call an old-fashioned mothering routine.

Navigating these somewhat awkward situations can be lonely and one cannot forget the son-in-law, who likely feels on the outer. These sorts of visits come from a place of love, willingness and sacrifice but are not without difficulties and tensions.

Later deliveries

Distinguished Professor Paul Spoonley stated in his recent publication, *The New New Zealand*, "[...] one of the most profound changes in the last 50 years has been the mother's age at the time of her first childbirth."

I have met grandparents whose distance daughters or daughters-in-law fell pregnant later in life while they, as grandparents-to-be, are in their twilight years. If it's the first grandchild, it can be an overwhelming place for the grandparent-to-be.

Rebecca and Jim (N.Z./England) have a blended family. They had one child together who was in his 40s when he and his partner had a child. Rebecca commented, "I never thought I would see a grandchild. I was 67 when she was born."

For others, they already had grown up in-country grandchildren, and they thought their hands-on grandparenting days were coming to an end.

> "To me it feels like I am a bit old to be a grandparent. I ought to be a great grandparent. That is the problem with our age. They've [our friends] got rid of all the [baby] equipment or they have moved to retirement villages. We're getting old and you just hope you are around long enough to see. We loved watching the boys [in-country grandsons] grow up and we don't know how long we will be able to watch Lisa [distance granddaughter] grow up. I want her to have New Zealandness. I want her to feel she can come here. Whether we'll be capable of looking after her when she is old enough to travel on her own, I don't know."
>
> Nancy (N.Z./England)

Twilight Distance Grandparenting is one of the things you have to take day by day and oftentimes you aren't sure *how* you will manage. Because your distance son and daughter don't see you face-to-face on a regular basis, they may have little appreciation you are feeling less energetic. On the flip side, they may decide you are too old to be left in charge of a little one, which is sad. My advice is to speak up. As parents *they* are worried about their new role and this is the time to be upfront that you might be worried too.

Babysitting and Childminding via Wi-Fi

Sometimes Distance Grandparents are left to briefly babysit by video. This involves a grandchild being convinced to sit still and the grandparent maybe reading them a book or having a one-on-one chat via a device, while the parent attends to a household task nearby or at the most basic level, has a moment to go to the toilet or read the newspaper in peace.

I have gone through phases of attempting to read a book via FaceTime to my toddler grandsons in America. Once, my daughter was trying to potty train the two-year-old. We convinced him to sit on the potty outside on the deck and she propped up the phone. I read a story book with my phone camera focused at my end on each page. Miraculously he sat still, did not mess with my daughter's phone and produced the goods. It was a red-letter day to be a Distance Grandmother.

This babysitting regime offers potential benefits to all parties; however, it is not necessarily an easy task for the grandparents. The grandparents enjoy less parental supervision of their calls but admit to sometimes asking too many questions, while other times not always knowing what to say. Additionally, toddlers left to their own devices would likely have their grandparent experiencing motion sickness from the constant handling of their parent's phone.

It is much easier to mind children who are a little older. When these sessions become a norm in the distance son or daughter's home, fantastic bonds can develop between grandparent and grandchild. Regular bedtime reading, interactive online games, singing, telling jokes and all manner of fun activities can give a parent a few minutes' relief.

Babysitters from Afar

If someone had suggested to me there would come a day when I would spend thousands of dollars to fly halfway around the world for the primary purpose of babysitting my grandchildren, while their parents needed to travel or work, I would have flatly dismissed the thought. But that's what I have done - evidence of the subtle, ongoing adjustments made by Distance Grandparents. Change is a constant companion.

Babysitting distance grandchildren delivers confusing emotions of obligation. On the one hand you (and I include myself here) can feel a bit worn out and physically challenged at times, constantly minding little ones, but on the other hand you know you have yearned for this opportunity and once you return home it will be all over again.

Attitudes to babysitting can be affected by cultural differences. There was consensus from some of Dr Holly Sevier's research participants (Indian grandparents living in Hawaii) that the possibility of needing to provide significant babysitting services during visits to their mainland U.S.A. family did not sit well with most of them. One grandfather commented, "I don't want to go there and just be a babysitter." In contrast though the grandmothers were always keen for any opportunity to teach their grandchildren how to cook traditional fare.

Most Distance Grandparents I've met are hands-on and do not expect to be waited on. They travel anticipating they have duties upon arrival and readily admit any visit is *not* a holiday.

The thought of babysitting alone when you haven't seen your grandchildren for some time can be daunting. Mark Silver and his wife travelled 2,000 miles from Maryland to Utah to babysit their one-and-a-half-year-old Jolene for a public holiday weekend. Mark reported, "In our 96 hours of solo grandparenting I learnt a lot about Jolene. I was reminded what it takes to be a good parent: in a nutshell, boundless energy [...] I'd forgotten parenting is exhausting. Those days of intense JoJo time made me love her even more, gave me a real feel for the rhythm of her days and nights and for her exuberant, take-charge personality. I left Utah loving her more than ever and eager for our next adventure in grandbabysitting. But I won't lie - the next day it was nice (and easy) to wake up with no baby responsibilities and head off to the office."

Ken and Nancy (N.Z./England) decided Nancy should travel to England for a babysitting assignment. The regular London child-minder was taking a two-week holiday in July and their daughter and son-in-law wanted to save up their work vacation leave for a New Zealand visit at Christmas. Nancy said, "I thought I would like to do this. We can afford for me to go over." Ken responded with, "So it's like a relief babysitter who happens to live 12,000 miles away." Later in the conversation Nancy commented, "I think my biggest fear when I am looking after her is, I am going to be in charge. I am to be the disciplinarian as well as the nice granny - grumpy granny - and... gosh, I hope she likes me."

When distance daughter Anna Seidel and her hubby were contemplating another global assignment, this time to Beijing, they arranged for Anna's mom, Peggy (Distance Grandmother), to fly from her home in the States to their current location, South Africa, so she could mind the children during their absence along with the support of their home help nanny, Patience. This enabled Anna and hubby to fly to Beijing for a *look and see* investigative trip. As explained by Anna, "We always find a way to get stuff done [...] Finding creative, workable solutions is one of my expat super-powers." Plus, of course, having a mother willing to co-operate.

It can be overwhelming to land and be presented with a to-do list. I can recall arriving to visit with little ones after a 16-hour overnight flight. Jet lag, adjustment to the tropical heat and upset sleep patterns are all par for the course for the first 48 hours. We were staying at an Airbnb, 10 minutes' walk away. I was advised that my daughter wanted to go to the 9.30 am yoga class the next morning and could we please be at the house in time. It could be said we should have spoken up but on the other hand we have flown all this way and haven't been with the grandchildren for months. Surely, we would want to jump at this opportunity? Selma Wassermann notes that distance family will at times push your boundaries and it pays to prepare ahead for how you will respond. As she advises: family members cannot read your mind. We should not expect them to do so.

Sometimes it can also be considered an honour to be asked to babysit. I remember a conversation with Maureen (N.Z./ East Coast U.S.A.) when she told me they had been asked to babysit their toddler granddaughter in America so the parents could take a brief, belated honeymoon and attend a wedding in London. There was no hesitation - their answer was 'yes'. The most powerful and overriding thought was she and her husband had been *asked*. They were being trusted with this little bundle and the grandparents wanted their son and daughter-in-law to have a break. The expense, time away from work and the demands of travel for the grandparents all dissipated as the honour of being trusted was overwhelming and felt like such a blessing. I spoke to Maureen and Ivan after this visit and they reported revelling in the nine days' alone time with their granddaughter.

The final babysitters-from-afar story I share below challenged me. I'm not sure how I would have reacted if I had been in their shoes.

During a visit to Atlanta, my husband and I met a lovely Australian Distance Grandparent farming couple who had just arrived to visit their family. The grandparents' journey from Australia took two days and involved four flights. Our journey a few days prior was bad enough, but theirs didn't bear thinking about. Their son is married to an American and at the time I think the local couple had six young children, including a baby. Their son is a passionate, zealous activist raising awareness about a serious social problem. The main purpose of the grandparents' visit was to babysit the children so their son and daughter-in-law could fly to Europe for an important commitment.

I admired the grandparents for being willing to take on this brood in a foreign city. However, when their son arrived at the airline check-in desk he was advised that his Australian passport had expired. There was no chance of acquiring a replacement in the time. The Europe trip never happened. It would be safe to assume the son had been so busy with his good works that keeping track of essential documentation had taken second place - a mistake anyone could make.

At the time I could not imagine how the grandparents felt. They were getting on in years and the journey over had taken its toll. If I was to put myself into their shoes, I wonder how gracious I would have been when I realised my son had let so many people down. In the end, they got to see a lot more of their son and daughter-in-law, which was a bonus and a blessing.

Rules and Routines

Few grandparents mentioned they have problems with grandparents' rules versus parents' rules. These situations can crop up, of course, but on the other hand if Distance Grandparents are lucky enough and sufficiently trusted to babysit their grandchildren, most times the middle generation is so grateful for their child-free break they are hardly going to complain. These are occasions when everyone realises one cannot be too black and white.

However, parenting involves constant tweaking and recalibrating. Rules and routines that applied on one visit may not be the default routine on the next visit. This can be a challenge for Distance Grandparents.

Doughnuts are a regular, purchasable, fundraising treat after some American church services. On one visit, doughnuts were a definite no-no from my health-conscious daughter and her toddler was distracted away from all such sugar-laden delicacies. I dutifully followed this regime on the next visit, explaining a doughnut was not a possibility; however, World War III erupted. Little did I know between visits the rules had changed and doughnuts were now a regular feature of post-church attendance. It seemed to take the rest of the day for our world to regain a sense of calm.

It wasn't as easy for this Distance Grandparent couple either. With the knowledge of a new language comes power. The daughter and family of friends of mine moved from New Zealand to Europe for a temporary work assignment. During the grandparents' first visit to Europe they babysat their three grandchildren for a week while the parents had a break. They thought this would be easy as they knew their grandchildren very well. However, the week proved unexpectedly challenging. The children, in just a few months, had acquired a proficient use of the local language - a language of which the grandparents had no knowledge. The children discovered they could have great fun being naughty (as the grandmother described) and speaking in their new language, causing no end of problems for the grandparents. My friends returned initially saying it was unlikely they would revisit next year.

A few months down the track, and a postscript to this story, I can report that flights are in place for *another* visit: a classic example of how swaying emotions and change are constant companions.

Surrogate/Honorary/Substitute Grandparents

Grandparents as surrogate parents is well documented - surrogate *grandparents,* less so. Surrogate grandparenting is a three-sided narrative with a comforting, win/win/win outcome. There are several reasons why this can be a good idea:

- The local surrogate grandparents are doing something that gives them fulfilment.
- The local distance son or daughter enjoys the safety net of a local caregiver.
- The Distance Parents/Grandparents know there is someone trying to fill a void they are unable to occupy themselves.

When Anna Seidel (American) was a child and living in Germany with her expat parents, she and her sister had a surrogate German grandmother. Anna's mother had met the local woman, who was older and single. Every Wednesday, when school finished at lunchtime, Anna and her sister would trot off happily to this woman's house for a meal. They were always served traditional German fare, played games and they would get picked up later. "That was an important relationship to us."

Distance Grandmother Valerie (Wales/Australia) has a niece with three children aged 7 to 14 years living close. The children have become surrogate grandchildren for her and she gains much from this relationship.

The following is my own story.

When Lucy lived in Bangkok she made a special friend with another young mother originally from Atlanta, Georgia. Coincidentally Lucy ended up moving to Atlanta. This friend's parents have gone on to become in-country, surrogate grandparents for my grandchildren and a precious emergency backstop babysitter for my daughter if work commitments and a sick child clash. They have also become treasured friends for my husband and me and are now part of our Atlantan grandparenting place. We have been entertained in their home and the two husbands are golfing buddies. Our friends always attend Grandparents' Day at our grandsons' preschool. One day a parcel and card arrived in the mail from Atlanta. The message read:

"Dear Helen and Clive,
I am sending you the note and ornament we got on Grandparents' Day at Peter's school. We have enjoyed looking at it and thinking of Peter, but felt it was meant for you and should move on to NZ! Enjoy!
Best regards, CC"

I admit to being just a dash envious of their local connection; however, that is completely different from being jealous and a normal emotion as mentioned in *Emotions and Loss, Acceptance and Resilience*. How Distance Grandparenting *is* for me, is significantly enhanced knowing these friends are hovering nearby my distance daughter. I am eternally grateful to have them part of our distance family package.

South African distance daughter Hendrika was aware of this dynamic when she regaled her surrogate role: "I have recently become a surrogate granny for two South African families here [Melbourne]. It is so hard. On the one hand you don't want the real granny to feel threatened but you also know these kids need somebody who can spoil them or read stories to them [in Afrikaans]."

My university professor who encouraged me to do my master's is herself a Distance Stepgrandmother with no children or grandchildren in New Zealand. When she retired, one of her new interests was making herself available to babysit the two children of her collegial replacement. This was a very welcome arrangement for a family setting up a home in a new country. My professor became a surrogate grandmother and the children adore her. When the Distance Grandmother from America visited, she expressed to me her heartfelt gratefulness for the role the professor had taken on. The professor positively bolstered how Distance Grandparenting was for the American Distance Grandmother.

Rosemary (N.Z./England) shared another delightful angle to this topic. When she travels to London, she takes time out to visit her New Zealand-based son's mother-in-law in Cornwall - another Distance Grandmother. Rosemary arrives with photos and videos of their shared New Zealand granddaughter and they enjoy a special time together. I loved hearing this thoughtful reverse Distance Grandparenting story.

A harder situation to navigate from afar is when, say for example, your distance daughter finds a sort of surrogate *mother* nearby, or your distance son connects with a *father* figure.

Peggy (East Coast U.S.A./Germany) recounted a situation with her distance single daughter who made friends with an older couple in the daughter's apartment block. The wife became a second mother to the distance daughter. Peggy's mature response to this new relationship remained one of gratefulness, but this reaction isn't instinctive for all.

Step/Blended Families

I've hesitated to highlight what some might call non-traditional family packages for the simple reason that Distance Grandparenting is unaffected. As Janet Teitsort explains in *long distance grandma*, "Love multiplies when you are blessed to be a grandparent not only to your biological children, but also to blended-in grandchildren."

Sometimes I wonder whether there are more blended families than traditional nuclear families! We are a blended family and know many others like us. There is a good chance many readers have stepgrandchildren.

As explained in *My Story* I became a stepgrandmother at 40. I definitely didn't want to be known as Nana, or similar: I was just Helen and remained Helen for our first batch of grandchildren. I did this for two reasons: I felt too young to be bestowed that title; and second, I didn't want to steal any limelight away from the biological grandmothers.

I can confirm titles do not matter. It is all about being there: how much you genuinely care and love those children is what matters. When it comes to Distance Grandparenting, from my experience it doesn't matter if you are *blood, blended* or *step* - the children, especially when they are young, aren't able to absorb the complexity of what the world deems a normal or abnormal family and, what's more, they don't care. In fact, one of the strengths of the Gen Z generation (those who have only ever known the internet - teenagers and those into their 20s - our older grandchildren) is their blanket acceptance and embracing of diversity and all it offers society.

EMOTIONS, BAD NEWS AND CRISES

---

*"Family crises have consequences for the parents
and children involved, but also for the grandparents
on both sides of the family."*
Maaike Jappens and Jay Van Bavel,
Journal of Marriage and Family

This final chapter on emotions is about the hard stuff. There is no escaping that once in a while life throws us all the odd curve ball, so grab the tissues. To Distance Grandparents who relate to a story or two here, I hope the written word gives you comfort that you are not alone. As we all know, bad things eventually pass and when you come out the other side the sun will shine again.

Worry

Worry is a default setting for Distance Parents and Distance Grandparents. I remember the following conversation from years ago with my daughter:

Skype call between New Zealand and South Sudan that disconnects itself every few minutes - audio only, no visuals, due to the intermittent weak connection.
Me: "What was that?"
Lucy: [under a mosquito net in her tent] "Gunfire - but it is a long way off. I probably should go now."

These days my family keep out of that form of harm's way but each time I travel with them on a freeway in the U.S.A., a narrow B road in the U.K., or ponder about my son who continues to ride Divvy rental bikes in Chicago, I am reminded that our lives could be turned upside down in a split-second and, yes, I worry about that.

> "I guess I worry because of being a mum. I worry about the fact I know the boys [three brothers] miss each other. They miss each other's company because they are very close." Later she surmised, when recounting a crucial visa processing problem her distance son was experiencing, "As long as things are going well for Nigel over there, I can feel reasonably calm and happy because I know it is going well for them. The minute they have these sorts of issues it kind of affects us again too. This is not good. So, you worry about it, and you're thinking about it. Gee, if they hadn't gone, they wouldn't have this problem."
>
> Maureen (N.Z./East Coast U.S.A.)

Distance Grandparents worry about situations and they worry about how their family experience these situations. Watching the daily news can be a minefield of anguish. A concerning story filmed in the city where your child lives may flash across the television screen. Naturally the Distance Grandparents begin to fret, while in actual fact the family is likely safely tucked up in bed, oblivious to what is going on.

The reality is *all* parents and grandparents worry and Distance Grandparents are no different, except their worry is experienced in a void - a worry that can be harder to tame.

Hearing Difficult News

There are times when distance children share news with their parents, that at the time they have no idea how impactful it is. Yes, the Distance Parents do know they have gone for good and as parents we like to think we are supportive. But there are some conversations Distance Grandparents and Distance Parents, including myself, will never simply just cruise through.

"My employer is arranging my permanent residency."

"I have an interview for my citizenship."

The logical, sensible part of oneself knows these are milestones to be celebrated. Dual citizenship, for example, is a privilege - for so many populations it's an impossible goal. However, momentarily such announcements represent another nail in the coffin of how you always *imagined* life would be.

Or what about this statement:

"I've arranged for [local friends] to be the children's guardians if I die."

This statement sends your mind into turmoil. *Why can't I look after my own grandchildren even if they do live in another country? There has got to be a way.* There are so many considerations to this decision, we all know, but it can cause heartache and as the Distance Grandparent, you can't bear to think about the *what ifs*.

In contrast to that scenario if an in-country son or daughter died and your local grandchildren became orphans you know there is a good chance the children would immediately end up under your roof. You could have an influence on their life outcome. You would pour love on them and manage somehow, even if you were getting on in years. A resilience would emerge you didn't know you possessed.

Why should it be different when geography forms part of the decision-making process? If your distance grandchildren *were* to live with a stranger's family, how on earth would you ever slot in as a grandparent? What an earthquake-shattering change for your grandchildren and what about the family taking them on?

These are what-if scenarios and thankfully I do not have real-life stories I can share.

Crises: The Toughest Test

Grandparents can play an important role in families undergoing stress or crisis. They can act as a stabilising force and a catalyst for wider family cohesion. A few Distance Grandparents and other friends asked me if I would be writing about coping with a family crisis from afar. "This is important," they would say. They did not necessarily have a personal crisis experience to contribute to my book but they felt it needed to be addressed.

One wintry day, when a smidgen of blue sky was trying to appear, I was pondering this question. I took a break from the computer and went to the garden centre. It wasn't yet spring but maybe a visit to the garden centre would sprinkle me with some spring-like feelings. While there, I bumped into a woman I only knew vaguely: we sing together in a local choir. She had some pansies in her trolley. "A little colour for a pot to brighten the day," she said.

We got talking, found out a bit more about each other and I learnt she was a Distance Grandmother also - twice over, like me, with family in the U.S.A. and England. When I shared with her my research/book project she also asked if I would be writing about crises. She told me right now she was worried about her English daughter-in-law who was going through rounds of chemotherapy and radiation therapy for breast cancer. "I so want to be there for them both but my daughter-in-law wants no one knocking at the door right now... and I can understand that," she said. "I am finding it very hard. I would like to read your book. I think I would be at home in it."

On the way home my thoughts were clarified: I knew I needed to address Distance Grandparenting (and Parenting) crises.

Rhonda and Colin (N.Z./Germany) shared a harrowing story of resilience, love and fortitude about their son in Europe, who at the time had three small children. This was many years ago, before the internet and today's ease of communication and travel.

One day Stuart, their distance son, rang from Germany and said, "I've got some bad news. I have got a brain tumour." Rhonda explained he knew the tumour was not malignant, but it needed to be removed. With little preparation or forethought for the consequences he was operated on and lost *all* his memory. He had recorded nothing beforehand and didn't know who he was. He convalesced in a hospital located in a town some distance from his wife, who was left to manage their young family. In the end Rhonda took herself off to Europe, to a country where she could not speak the language, to be at his bedside. Armed with photo albums and old letters she helped him regain some of his memory.

A few months later, still with little or no short-term memory, he flew by himself halfway around the world to visit his parents. An act they described as defying comprehension. Their son slowly rebuilt his life, as best he could. Talk of this son still easily initiates tears for Rhonda.

Similarly, I recall twice dropping everything for distance family crises. The first time was a few years ago. Suddenly, it felt like everything else in life was unimportant, including the tail end of a university semester's study. I hastily submitted my assignments ahead of deadlines and missed the last two weeks of class.

Lucy and family had moved from Thailand to live permanently in the U.S.A. After temporarily living with the in-laws, they moved interstate to the city where they were settling, to an empty house they had just purchased. My daughter was eight months pregnant with a toddler in tow in a new city. Unexpectedly, our son-in-law had to travel abroad with his work. Back in New Zealand our neighbour's daughter had just delivered at eight months. *What if this happens to my daughter?* we fretted. The scenario was frightening.

My husband and I were already booked to visit for the due date, to mind the toddler, but overnight my flight reservation was brought forward and I was on a plane, ahead of my husband. As it was, baby arrived two weeks late, at the very end of our visit, and we had just a couple of days to enjoy him! By the time I returned home two months later I admit I was well and truly past my use-by date as a Distance Mother and Distance Grandmother.

Separation and Divorce: Emotions on Steroids

Although there are blended married couples amongst the Distance Grandparents featured in this book and some of the single Distance Grandmothers are also divorced, the memories of relationship trials and tribulations are in the past for them all and their current relationships are stable and secure. A couple of grandparent couples I have interviewed had experienced divorce within their distance children's marital relationships; however, we did not dwell on this during our interviews as it had occurred many years ago.

In this section I will discuss separation and divorce of the distance middle generation and its effect on Distance Grandparents. Here I am challenged as it is my own family package that can shed light on contemporary separation and divorce within this generation - not once... but twice. I relate to a comment by Ruth Behar in *The Vulnerable Observer: Anthropology That Breaks Your Heart* when she notes, "Nothing is stranger than this business of humans observing other humans in order to write about it." She goes on to comment that what happens within the observer, in this case... me, must be made known.

Separation and divorce within any generation can have significant ramifications for all family members. When geographical distance is added to the mix and physical contact is problematic, there is another layer of grief, loss and heartache: an extreme example of how Distance Grandparenting *is*.

For this reason, and as much as I hesitate to share my dirty washing, I am including, with the blessing of my family, stories and reflections of crises and separation/divorce within my middle generation. This is not easy, but at the same time I've asked myself the question, *Will there ever be another occasion when a researcher/writer, who is also a Distance Grandparent, experiences a series of events similar to mine and be willing and able to share their family traumas?* While Distance Grandparent research remains scarce on the ground, I include my own trials and tribulations to enable readers to experience first-hand the topic's conflicts and emotions.

Lucy's marriage was always tenuous and she and our son-in-law would readily admit this now. Communication in all forms was difficult, much of the time. Visits to Bangkok and later Atlanta to see them and our two toddler grandsons were strained and stressful for my husband and me. When our daughter phoned and tearfully announced her marriage was over, we were deeply shocked. Despite everything this was completely unexpected.

During that time, she became very sick coping with events. For the second time I dropped everything and flew over, by myself, for three weeks. It was incredibly stressful and at times a lonely visit.

The state of Georgia allows a divorce to be filed 30 days from the date of separation. In New Zealand we are accustomed to a two-year compulsory wait. Watching this all unfold at a record pace was unnerving. The ongoing months were testing. It was a whirlwind of emotions, big decisions, long video calls and emails mixed in with giant adjustments and bucketloads of acceptance.

My autobiographic thoughts on divorce do not stop with my daughter. While writing my university thesis, my Distance Step-parenting and Step-grandparenting world was unexpectedly turned upside down again, just a year after Lucy's divorce. It was during this time I truly felt I was living my thesis. Everywhere I looked and everything I thought was focused on distance family flux.

My stepson Guy and his family in England communicated spasmodically - it worked both ways. We always connected on birthdays and Christmas but regular back and forth emails and Skype calls were not the norm; however, we made many visits to them. This was not because there was no desire to communicate - it was simply tricky and problematic. His children (our grandchildren) have never visited New Zealand.

Then out of the blue we got a text from Guy asking if we could talk at a particular time the next day. This was unusual. We connected and found him in the depth of despair. He's a very steady personality: a 50-something, ever patient, brick-wall kind of man. The call was littered with upset, gut-wrenching despair and he admitted his 22-year-old marriage was likely over.

Shortly after we flew to Fiji for a week's holiday. It was during that visit we received another text to confirm the marriage was over and 'could we chat?' We were lying by the pool and a long walk from our room. My husband and I shared one half of a set of headphones we happened to have with us and talked quietly via WhatsApp into my phone so the neighbouring bathers could not hear. He was bereft and so were we. My concern immediately shifted to our then 17 and 20-year-old distance grandchildren, whose lives had been irreversibly turned upside down, never to return to the former status quo. I knew they would never forget this day. My heart ached for the whole family.

Fiji is dotted with tiny isolated islands. We were at a resort surrounded by hundreds of guests and staff. My husband and I might as well have been stranded on a desert island - there was nothing we could do on the other side of the world. Later that day, across the coconut tree, palm-filled expanse of the Pacific Ocean fringed lawn, a Fijian band was singing at the seafood buffet extravaganza. We ate in.

The next day I wrote, "I don't know what to do with myself. I am on holiday in paradise and supposed to be celebrating our 30th wedding anniversary. I am so sad about the family and my eyes keep welling up with tears. I don't know what to think or feel. It should all be wonderful here, but it isn't. I feel very lonely."

Picking up the pieces

"It is not necessarily the divorce itself that has the potential to cause the most damage but it is uncertainty of what lies ahead."
Ann Thomas and Lauren Bovington, *The International Family Law Group, ExpatChild*

As I write this book both distance family separation journeys are moving and swaying in a positive direction. However, when I walk up and down the hallway at my home, I am constantly reminded I need to somehow, sometime, replace wedding photos in the family gallery. Our things have been messed with.

How will all this affect our relationship with both sets of distance grandchildren? These insecurities and confused responsibilities fuel a worried busyness of our brains questioning what we should or should not do. Likewise, our connections with our son-in-law and our daughter-in-law will likely take a gradual decline. We care for them and it doesn't sit right.

We also have connections with the respective parents-in-law, who live in-country, reasonably convenient to our distance family. We used to enjoy their company on visits, revelling in our common denominator grandchildren. We have known them for many years and we sense a loss there also.

We have become co-Distance Grandparents. Lucy has her small boys only 50% of the time so consequently our opportunities to communicate with these grandchildren are halved. Furthermore, we have had to accept there may come a time when she visits New Zealand... by herself, because it is, for example, her ex-husband's turn to have the children at Christmas.

Sociologists Sara Arber and Virpi Timonen in *Contemporary grandparenting* talk of divorce in the middle generation resulting in role transitions and 'reconstituted families'. We have experienced bucketloads of transition and in time may become further reconstituted if our daughter and/or son acquire a new partner and maybe even more children.

Invisible Grandparenting

For some, divorce and other family traumas result in making family connections tricky and awkward. This can occur for many reasons from simple apathy to ingrained bitterness.

Here's an email from my daughter referring to her Australian-residing biological dad, my ex-husband, who has not been prominent in her life: "Heard from G today. He asked the 'delicate' question: 'I'm not even sure what I'm saying but... just want to check how you feel about me being in the boys' lives? Ya know, having to explain who I am and...' And of course I told him he was always welcome. I said, Life's short, don't miss out on any more. Give me a buzz in the morning and if we're good to chat I'll answer in more detail."

Worse still, estrangement occurs - cutting completely any connection with their grandchildren. This is a huge step further than a difficult *gatekeeper* distance son or daughter. *Invisible Grandparenting* is the title of a book by Dr Pat Hanson, who was twice-over an estranged grandmother. These circumstances are tragic, overwhelming and devastating for anyone who lives with them. I can highly recommend her book. She shared a daily meditation that might be useful to affected Distance Grandparents:

"When we focus on what we are missing, we are focusing on lack, loneliness, longing and loss of some kind. The energy of that focus is really poisonous, diminishes our relationships, makes us sad, and generally brings more unhappy experiences to us. I discovered that whenever I feel myself missing my family, my grandbabies, my friend, if instead I gave thanks for those people I loved so deeply, I felt better. The sadness would leave and in its place, the appreciation for my life grew. In most cases the love grew, connections deepened, and I discovered a great gift: love knows no borders, barriers, or conventional distinctions. Love is love is love. Let the active art of not missing give you its gift. I am so grateful."
Rev. Barbara Leger cited in *Invisible Grandparenting*

Emotions: Final Advice

In reviewing the four chapters on emotions and reflecting on how Distance Grandparenting *is* for grandparents, some-times... it is tough. The topics have provided a glimpse into the trials and tribulations some Distance Grandparents experience.

Those of us featured found that the periods of worry and crisis profoundly affected our health and well-being and were lonely, worrisome journeys. Even the best of local friends find it hard to comprehend how it felt and nobody wants to hear your woes repeated too often.

So what have I learnt about distance family crises and is there advice I can share? I recommend four action steps.

1. **Don't journey alone.**
   Your mind and body will take an attack - none of us is programmed to counteract that. Panic attacks, lack of sleep and anxiety are likely constant bedfellows. Make an appointment with your doctor and fill him or her in.
2. **Know you can't fix it.**
   Whatever has happened, likely the best you can do is listen without judgement. When advice is requested - give it. When it isn't - hold it back.
3. **Repeat to yourself, *this will pass*.**
4. **Consider consulting an expert.**
   A Family Psychologist/Counsellor will arm you with techniques to ride out the storm or adjust your focus. Find one locally or if you are struggling to locate a psychologist with an understanding of global families check the *Resources* section for international contacts. These experts are accustomed to counselling remotely and you'll be surprised how easy it is to connect.

Lastly, if you are one half of a Distance Grandparent couple, work at being on the same page. If ever there is a time your distance family need to know you are a secure unit it is now.

If you are new to Distance Grandparenting please be assured life is *not* usually this drama-filled. Most Distance Grandparents have harmonious family relationships and never touch on the topics I have raised. Life is filled with savoured, photographed, frivolous, fun-filled times which we're constantly reminded of when the miracles of the FaceTime algorithms generate anniversary posts and photo collection videos.

RITUALS AND TRADITIONS

"Maintaining and adding to rituals picked up along our journeys reflect the places we've been and the people we've loved."
Linda A. Janssen, *The Emotionally Resilient Expat*

Most families have rituals and traditions, so what is significant about distance family rituals? Rituals form points of connection, a sense of security for all generations. They awaken and remind the senses of connections, places and people: a valuable, soothing conduit to lessen the distance. For Distance Grandparents, rituals have power and can shift and change at each visit. These rituals and traditions, no matter how small, are clung to like a closely guarded cuddly rug.

> **66** Distance Grandparenting rituals and traditions, no matter how small, are clung to like a closely guarded cuddly rug. **99**

Food

Food traditions and rituals are centre stage for distance families.

Before any family visit (in either direction) grandparents go shopping. Certain food items are top of the list. Great effort, expensive luggage allowance and determined shopping expeditions are afforded treasured gourmet fare. Eyes light up and mouths water when cherished treats emerge from suitcases.

> "We would always take Gingernut biscuits [cookies] and Crunchie bars."
>
> (Maureen N.Z./East Coast U.S.A.)

Yorkshire teabags and chocolate covered ginger biscuits from Marks and Spencer were frequently mentioned by U.K. based Peter Gosling. Cecile from Canada has transported her country's famous maple syrup from Quebec to both Norway and Cambodia, along with homemade rhubarb pineapple jam.

There is probably no more iconic a New Zealand taste and smell sensation than the vegetable extract product Marmite. On our last U.S.A. visit we carried eight large jars. I suspect the reason one suitcase missed a connection was due to the dense jars of Marmite which likely attracted the attention of the American Aviation Environment Federation. After already travelling 19 hours we had to wait at the airport another hour or so for the next flight, which delivered the missing bag and suspicious contents.

When travelling to the U.K. we have to carry a particular sherbet sweet which can only be bought here. While I was writing this chapter a request was made via Skype: "Please send some fizzy lollies."

Baking

Rhonda (N.Z./Germany) is a very capable cook, gardener and seamstress. When I asked if her family had any food traditions she promptly replied, "As long as there is plenty of cake. Everyone likes Grandma's baking."

I am no baker like Rhonda; however, I am known for my old family recipe fruitcake. I gingerly attempted to pass on a love of this treat to my American grandsons who live in a country that has little appreciation of this delicious English pleasure. It is no exaggeration to say these young lads have become obsessed with fruitcake so it is transported in suitcases (with the Marmite) to America. It has even achieved the lofty status of Santa's favourite indulgence. A slice is left under the tree on Christmas Eve along with the English tradition of a glass of port.

This senses-filled (sight, taste and smell) fruitcake experience for my grandsons has evolved into an embedded family tradition and builds bonds and connections while simultaneously trying to offset the unsettling nature of Distance Grandparenting. Fruitcake is a working partner in my Distance Grandparenting role.

Cooking for family

Grandparents comment that they miss cooking for and hosting family gatherings. Having all your family sit around the same table is a much-cherished, out of reach luxury for most Distance Grandparents. They are a chance to share ethnic and favourite childhood dishes. These times lessen anxiety and keep connections alive. One mouthful at a time a life imagined is savoured and temporarily the distance doesn't feel as vast.

The last time this occurred for my husband and me was in 2009 in New Zealand. One child lived nearby and the others arrived from Dunedin (N.Z.), London and South Sudan. It was a case of *good luck* rather than *good management* that our four children were in the same city and country at the same time. We enjoyed just one treasured evening meal together, sitting around our dining table. I have no idea if, or when, this will ever happen again.

"You miss a lot of fun, a lot of relationships. It is not like you can sit down and eat together."
Hannah (England/Switzerland and U.S.A.)

Similarly, family reunions, especially with grandchildren, are also just about an impossibility. This was mentioned by Walter and Sandra (South Africa/Australia and U.S.A.). Three of their five children live abroad. "One thing we miss is the fact that owing to all the different circumstances of our children and grandchildren and different situations regarding work conditions, we are not able to arrange a simultaneous family reunion with our local children and the overseas children," Walter said. "However, we have accepted the fact and have dealt with that in our relations with them. We do not expect much change in the future. We are accepting it as a fact of life."

One of the advantages of utilising self-catering Airbnbs when you travel, is being able to invite family over for a meal. Sharing the cooking duties between two kitchens adds a brilliant dynamic to a family visit.

Detachable Bundles of Practices

Author and Anthropologist Katy Gardner studies 'sending' communities, which means the left behind family of contemporary, long-term migration, like Distance Grandparents. Together with the late Emeritus Professor of Social Anthropology, Ralph Grillo (1947-2016), formerly from the University of Sussex, they explain rituals are neither static events nor a static process. They label rituals as 'detachable bundles of practices'. What a delightful analogy. Even the tiniest act or item offers much comfort to Distance Grandparents.

My husband and I have a habit when we go out of leaving our slippers at the bottom of the stairs in readiness for our return. One day when Guy was visiting from the U.K. shortly after his separation, the men left for an outing. When I was home, I noticed *two* pairs of male slippers on the stairs. This little ritual became a comforting sight of a relaxed family visit. I wonder when the visiting slippers will reappear.

Rhonda (N.Z./Germany) regaled stories of particular plants purchased to recognise the birth of each grandchild and how these plants reflected the personality of each one. The plants have been moved, re-potted and transported during house moves and still have a home in Rhonda's current residence. "Felicity's is a dainty little water lily and you know it is just like Felicity - very beautiful with everything in its place," she said. When visiting grandchildren arrive they immediately search out *their* plant. Despite the physical absence of Felicity, her presence is felt in the water lily.

Rhonda also sewed a new set of pyjamas, or nightdress, for her distance grandchildren's visits. These items were so loved the children were often seen wandering down the street in their new and much-admired night apparel.

Detachable bundles of practice are taken to a whole new level by Jill (N.Z./England). Her family's heart-stirring tradition below will leave you with a sense of awe.

Jill's son and his family work around the world, returning to New Zealand at times. When her grandson was born in New York she brought home the newborn's *whenua* (placenta) and buried it under a tree at a special spot on a Tairāwhiti (East Coast) beach. When her granddaughter was born, her whenua was buried alongside that of her brother in a family ceremony. While a tradition for Māori (New Zealand indigenous race), many others in New Zealand, like Jill's family are also claiming this practice. Burying the whenua reinforces a physical, spiritual and familial link to the land. A stone marks the spot and this is a place of belonging for her grandchildren. It will never be forgotten as GPS coordinates are recorded and represent a place in her children's transitory worlds - that will never change.

Things

The charm of detachable bundles of practice spills over into everyday things. The meaning and history of particular treasured objects can impact and deliver strong connections for distance families.

Daniel Miller is an Anthropologist at the University College of London and has written a couple of books called *Stuff* and *The Comfort of Things*. He is interested in the relationship of humans to their things. This is called 'material culture', or 'materiality'. He explains it this way: "Objects store and possess, take in and breathe out the emotions with which they have been associated."

In *The Comfort of Things*, Miller visited various homes in a North London street analysing residents' household items. He read much into the lives of his participants by analysing their things. Things can demonstrate identity. I was startled when he made a statement, based on extensive research, that people who have developed meaningful relationships to things often forge meaningful relationships with people. However, those who fail at one, often fail at the other. This is a bold statement, and for me the jury remains out. Decluttering later in life can be incredibly freeing. Despite this Miller has, however, awakened my thoughts and appreciation of the potential value of things.

Boxes feature in Peggy's (East Coast U.S.A./Germany) Distance Grandparenting efforts. When each grandchild turns five she sends a special box full of small items all commencing with letters from the child's name. "I now know I need to start each birthday box about a year in advance," Peggy said. "This delights me as I have that particular grandchild on my mind all the time. Everywhere I go, every shop I enter, each time I'm online I am looking for objects starting with certain letters. Often I have to make an object myself [examples: apron, valentine]." Once the items are gathered she then writes a story featuring the items and creates a book. "My daughter reports her children still like to get out their box now and then and look at the little objects - even the 12-year-old."

Boxes feature again in the story below.

I once transported in my suitcase a precious heirloom christening gown (first sewn for me). Even the box it was carried in held significance. The cardboard carton is around 60 years old and was a freebie decades earlier from my grandfather's funeral director business - the packaging for new coffin handles. I experienced a strange feeling of embodiment (a concrete form to an abstract idea) being responsible for this heirloom (box and all), away from the safety of New Zealand. It was hard to relax until it was returned home to my mother, the great grandmother and seamstress.

Amongst the stuff at my house is an assorted stash of kiddie gear and toys. A stair barrier resides under the guests' bed, board games live at the top of a wardrobe and a port-a-cot, retro highchair (bought for me!), ride on bike, bashed about plastic table and chairs and other toys reside, off and on, in our attic roof space. I find this stuff comforting and, what's more, I can share it with local friends when their distance family come to stay.

Also stashed away are the Christmas tree decorations. Each December we are reminded of family visits as foreign decorations waken memories of past journeys and connections.

Books are powerful things of Distance Grandparenting. Particular children's books and story characters instantly remind me of certain visits to grandchildren.

Sixteen years later, I can still visualise the low-ceilinged rooms of a quintessential thatched cottage in Dorset where we holidayed with our family. Thomas the Tank Engine reigned supreme. James, Percy, Edward and Gordon were all there and let's not forget the Fat Controller.

A New Zealand author, Betty Gilderdale, has written a children's series for which a yellow digger is the main character. I remember the *Yellow Digger* visit to Atlanta. Nearby in the neighbourhood much construction was happening and every day I would bundle my wee grandson into a blue wagon with a wobbly wheel and we'd haphazardly venture forth to soak up the action. Peter would sit on the verge mesmerised taking in every digger manoeuvre. As a result, supplies of new *Yellow Digger* books have been transported to the States so our grandson could give them as birthday presents to his friends. The *Yellow Digger* is right at home in Atlanta.

Later came the true adventure of a young New Zealand man called Brando Yelavich who walked around the coast of our country: an epic journey of craziness. His book, *The Wild Boy*, has become iconic in our distance familying. What's more my husband and I happen to know Brando's parents. They live nearby and sometimes we bump into them. Twice I have embarrassingly asked for a selfie with them. We have achieved super-hero status because we know Brando's mum and dad and our selfie photos adorn our grandson's bedroom wall. When we travel around New Zealand I buy postcards of coastal scenes and airmail them to the boys. On the reverse I write: 'Wild Boy walked here'.

Photos

Photos are the pinnacle of things. They are an important visual reminder of distance family: pride of place frames, arranged on a coffee table or randomly adorning a refrigerator door secured with tourist magnets acquired from here and there.

In years gone by, when a film canister was full, it was automatically taken to the chemist for printing. When our first grandchildren were born, any self-respecting grandparent at that time owned a *brag book* - a small photo album featuring a selection of show-off baby photos. These days photos are saved on phones and iPads. (Perhaps photos around the home are less common?) Grandchildren feature in my mobile phone wallpaper. Have our phones, to some extent, replaced the mantelpiece?

The digital age has made it relatively easy to produce photo memory books. Photo developing companies everywhere offer this service. I have compiled many over the years and airmailed them to my grandchildren as a visual taste of an upcoming visit or a reminder of a recent visit. Glimpsing well-thumbed versions in the toy box during visits warms my heart. When you cannot be there photos help bridge the gap, reinforce memories and maintain family bonds.

My research unearthed one home where the photo display was particularly prominent and demonstrated the overwhelming love and devotion Jim and Rebecca (N.Z./England) have for their distance granddaughter. Three pride of place, large framed photos dominated the dresser in the centre of the lounge room and a bedroom had been beautifully decorated with a *Frozen* movie theme for a recent visit. This effort included a wallpaper mural imported from England, matching curtains, duvet cover and many other movie décor accessories. The grandparents had lovingly executed all the DIY handiwork. Their Skype conversations are conducted here so the granddaughter can see her room via a mirror on the opposite wall displaying a reflection of the mural. The love these grandparents have for their granddaughter is overflowing and this beautiful bedroom felt like a shrine to her absence. We joked as we hoped she did not fall out of favour with *Frozen* as this decorating masterpiece had been a huge effort for the grandparents.

Parcels in the mail

In this digital age who doesn't enjoy opening a parcel adorned with stamps or postage labels, all the while resisting the temptation to read the customs declaration? Postage seems such a waste of money when for just a small charge you can arrange for Amazon, or similar, to deliver from close by. But it isn't the same.

Many countries make receiving parcels problematic and expensive. The United Kingdom, for example, charges the recipient VAT and Customs Duties based on the value of the contents as noted on the customs declaration form. What example are we to our distance family if we tell fibs about the content's value so as to avoid the attention of Custom's officials? The anticipation of the parcel's contents definitely loses its shine when a VAT invoice is received by the participant or worse still the parcel goes missing. After three decades of sending birthday and Christmas parcels to the United Kingdom we have near enough given up as our family has been presented with invoices from Customs to receive our packages.

Pets

Pets are also detachable bundles of practices: moving, loving things of distance familying. In *Key Findings: The How It Is* I detailed the different places of Distance Grandparenting. Pets, in a way, also deserve the status of a place of distance familying.

Stories of a much-loved family pet offer a longitudinal view of distance familying. In the context of Distance Grandparenting they encapsulate so much of what has been discussed: absence, presence, the senses, traditions, rituals, loss, grief and acceptance. They offer a place of belonging for distance family.

Willow

I have stayed with Distance Grandparents Rhonda and Colin (N.Z./Germany) and it was during these visits I was introduced to their corgi, Willow. She was an important part of their daily routine and the devotion from them and the dog in return was evident. My husband and I, despite our ambivalence towards pets, took a liking to Willow. Rhonda and Colin explained to me what Willow meant to their in-country *and* distance grandchildren.

Colin: A couple of nights ago, when they [in-country family] came back from overseas, one of the boys [grandson]... the only thing he wanted to know was 'how's Willow?'.
Rhonda: And every dog we've ever had has been very important to the grandchildren. We're on the third one [dog] now with grandchildren.

Colin and Rhonda have had a few house moves. While their home hasn't been a consistent anchor for their grandchildren, Willow has provided an agency of stability. Willow is a steadfast place of their distance familying.

It came as a shock, just three weeks after my research visit, when I received an email reading, "Willow died yesterday. She had a liver collapse. We are a bit distraught about her but will get ourselves together soon." Even as a non-doggie person, I was upset.

A few weeks later I asked Rhonda how the extended family had reacted and how they were coping with Willow's passing. In her email she wrote, "The answer is the grandchildren were very upset. Three crying [in-country] children on the yacht in the Pacific. Susan [distance granddaughter] sent an email of sympathy [from Europe] along the lines of a death in the family, enumerating Willow's nice characteristics. Stuart [distance son] was very upset and the local [N.Z.] family was very supportive because they had the same thing [death of a pet] a year ago. 'Death in the Family' was the theme. Everyone was very upset we were not going to get another dog. They should have known better and so should we. In due course, dog number four, called Breezee, was acquired which has met with approval from all quarters." Willow and now Breezee are steadfast anchors and non-negotiable conduits of place of Rhonda and Colin's distance familying.

A dog called LB

Another doggie story, this time geographically reversed, deeply impacted Glennis Annie Browne (N.Z./Australia and Indonesia). "Being a Distance Parent and Grandparent for me includes the precious, much-loved pets of my children," Glennis said. "Just now I called my son, who lives overseas, who this afternoon had to call the vet to end the suffering of his 16-year-old Labrador called LB. To hear your adult son sobbing on the end of the phone is heart-wrenching. When he said 'This is the hardest thing I have ever done', I felt his pain. We as parents, wear our hearts on our sleeve, suffering as our children suffer. This is what being human means to me. This is love."

Rituals and Traditions: a Final Reflection

The common denominator to all the stories in this chapter is the most insignificant act, thing or practice - whether it is a particular cardboard box, a photo in the mail or a cookie from the supermarket - each has meaning and its own back story. Creating traditions and continuously working at those rituals is one of the valuable roles of Distance Grandparenting. While our distance sons or daughters might be so busy just getting through each day, we can quietly take it upon ourselves to gently encourage these detachable bundles of practice.

VISITS

One day while sitting in an airport departure lounge I jotted down this poem:

> *Family come... family go - intense visits when*
> *all senses are on alert.*
> *Noise, activity and general mayhem all halted at the*
> *airport's All Gates sign...*
> *Drawn out, eerily quiet, in-between, private empty voids.*

Baldassar et al. in *Families Caring Across Borders* surmise that for most people, most of the time, visits are quintessentially a blessing and people greatly enjoy them.

Journeys in either direction are focal points on the distance familying calendar and add to the discourse of a multi-sited place for Distance Grandparents. Some visits include regular Northern Hemisphere summer pilgrimages while for others there are the obligatory Christmas rendezvous. For most there are no hard and fast patterns around how visits are planned. Romanian Sociologists Ionuţ Földes and Veronica Savu noticed this and referred in their *Studia UBB Sociologia* article to the fluid comings and goings as both 'multidirectional and asymmetrical'. I would also add, sometimes they are particularly productive. Once my husband and I managed to visit all three of our distance children's families on the same continent, albeit across three American states, when the U.K. family crossed the Atlantic and hit the theme parks of Florida. It felt like a gold star Distance Grandparenting travel achievement.

Reason and Nature of Visits

Baldassar et al. tidily categorise visits in either direction under two sets of criteria.

The first relates to the *reason for a visit*, which is influenced by three variables:

1. Capacity, ability and issues of time and money.
2. Obligation or a sense of duty.
3. Negotiated commitments - what has been established as the historical norm for a distance family regarding who does, or does not visit, and how often.

The second, *the nature of the visit*, falls into five categories:

1. **Routine visits**
   The primary motivation is to visit and be with family. The likely venue is a family home but perhaps a geographically central meeting point. I have, for example, holidayed with our U.K. distance family in the Netherlands, France, U.S.A. and various locations in England.
2. **Crisis visits**
   Urgent visits for a specific reason.
3. **Duty and ritual visits**
   Life-cycle visits often around the likes of a wedding or christening.
4. **Times of transition**
   Visits might be for the birth of a child, the final stages of a terminal illness or reasons of homesickness.
5. **Tourist visits**
   Family visits in conjunction with a tourist-focused holiday. The family visit on this occasion is more likely a stopover, or side-trip, in between other plans - a way to connect

with family, without staying for an extended length of time. Extended family, rather than immediate family, more often fit this category.

Distance families' reasons for visiting in either direction and the nature of their visits fall into these categories and frequently there is a crossover. Many examples have already been mentioned. These categories are helpful to think about as they highlight the flexibility and investment required by *all* parties regarding *who* will travel and who will *host*, *why* a visit is planned and *where* it might occur. It is also a reminder of the many trips that are helpful to maintain physical family connections. Counter to this, the list exposes what is being missed by those who cannot or choose not to travel.

Is Travel a Cultural Thing?

How eager and/or willing are Distance Grandparents from different countries to travel to visit their family? This is an interesting question. It is difficult to make a definitive argument either way so instead I will share the evidence I have gathered. These factors offer good reasons why some nationalities *might* be more willing, or able, to travel than others.

Nature of contract

The first consideration has to be the contract or work assignment of the distance son or daughter in question. As explained in *Unpacking Distance Grandparenting* the nature of the distance child's (or their partner's) employment contract can have a profound effect on whether Distance Grandparents embrace the idea of travelling or not.

Expat distance sons and daughters, with back-to-back, on-the-move, two-to-three-year international assignments frequently, but not always, receive an annual travel allowance to fund an annual visit to their homeland. Naturally, when this is the case Distance Grandparents are going to take a back seat and willingly host, rather than travel to somewhere that could be out of their comfort zone. Despite the obvious benefits to all parties, after a period of time, the distance son or daughter may long for their parent or parents to visit them, creating a year off from the annual pilgrimage.

In contrast, when there is no annual travel package and both the Distance Grandparents and distance son and daughter are on their own financially, questions around willingness to travel are on an even playing field.

Old-fashioned courtesies

In previous generations it was customary and expected for younger family members to make the pilgrimage to visit elderly, out of town grandparents, instead of the other way around. Grandparents didn't travel as they do today and, of course, their life expectancy wasn't as bright as seniors enjoy now. It is possible there's a hanging-on of this old tradition and an expectation that today's grandparents deserve the same treatment as they bestowed upon their own grandparents. This is the exception to the rule, I believe, but may exist in some quarters.

Holiday/vacation employment allowances

Another cultural issue sits around annual employment leave allowances. Significant disparity exists between holiday/vacation allowances extended to, for example, Americans compared to much of the rest of the Western world. In the States the annual allowance can be as little as two weeks and employees are frequently discouraged from taking it all in one go. This means extended overseas travel isn't possible for working Americans until their retirement years by which time it might all feel daunting and foreign, resulting in an ambivalence to travel and a preference for staying home.

In comparison, Australians and New Zealand citizens enjoy four weeks' annual leave. Employers are sympathetic to the need to travel and will try and allow leave to be taken all at once and will even consider carrying over annual leave from one year to the next to create an extended break.

What's nearby?

Anna Seidel, an expat coach and a distance daughter living in Germany, considered how a home location, with plenty to offer nearby, offered little incentive to get on a plane and travel halfway around the world. "If you live in mainland Europe, you don't have to go anywhere," she said. "You can drive or train to so many destinations. The concept of getting on a plane and travelling is foreign. Similarly, America is huge. So you don't have to travel to get to places to enjoy diversity. The mindset of travelling is culturally dependent." If annual leave is in short supply then a holiday/vacation down the road is a likely choice and may be the only option.

Passport statistics

Passport statistics reflect the trends above. The U.S. State Department estimates 42% of the population possess a passport (VOA News). However, 70% of New Zealand's population has a passport (Wikipedia) and 60% in Australia (Gebicki). These sorts of statistics illustrate varied attitudes to embracing international travel.

In conclusion, is travelling to see distance family, from the grandparents' perspective, a cultural thing or simply a case that there are factors at play for some nationalities, hindering a mindset that long haul family visits are normal? I believe it is a combination of all the above. The willingness or otherwise to travel is both a cultural thing and a by-product of factors over which Distance Grandparents frequently have little control.

Finally, travel and visits in either direction cost money. This is a big subject and is covered all in one go in a later chapter called *Uncertainty.*

VISITS: THEY VISIT HOME

"She has this very clean house, and everything is in its order and then I come through like a tornado with my two young active boys and everything gets put upside down and it's a whirlwind."
Sundae Schneider-Bean, *Expat Happy Hour*

The only thing better than visiting family overseas is them visiting home. Most Distance Grandparents agree here. It still feels like a monumental undertaking, but this time it's happening on *your* turf and you're able to sleep in *your* bed.

Emotions are high. You have cleaned, rearranged the house to suit, shopped at the supermarket in a way you never normally do, dug out toys from the attic and gone to the library for extra children's reading material. You've been on the phone or online and bought or borrowed car seats, stroller, cot, door barriers, highchair or whatever is essential to equip your house for the onslaught. When the day comes and they first appear in the Arrivals Hall you melt in a blubbering mess.

Once home, it doesn't take two minutes before the normally calm, adults-only-zone house is overrun with noise, mayhem and mess! Shouting, crying and jet-lagged whining - toys and stuff everywhere like aliens have landed and, what's more, there's nowhere to retreat. We all want the family to come but this is the reality and, as it has been said before, 'we wouldn't want it any other way'.

But there are two sides to every story of course. The visiting family has their own agenda. Some desperately want to catch up with old friends while the grandparents just want time with them. Others see catching up with extended family as a chore and a bore and a waste of their precious annual leave; however, these obligations need to be attended to. Furthermore, *home* means so many different things to them. It is lovely to be there but stifling in other ways. Our distance children are used to their new country and they no longer feel at home in what was their home. Or maybe the family home was sold years ago and the grandparents' current home comes with no memories: it's just a place to stay. It's a balancing act for the visiting family and a balancing act for the host grandparents.

> **"It's a balancing act for the visiting family and a balancing act for the host. "**

Finally, Distance Parents need to be prepared to take turns about how often their children visit. As Rhoda (distance daughter in Switzerland with her mother in the U.K.) reminds us, "Intercultural relationships are on the rise. Your married child is juggling visits to their homeland and their partner's homeland(s). Three or more countries are involved in intercultural marriages."

Putting on a Hotelier's Hat

My travel industry experience has caused me to be a tad picky about little things. When you are setting up a guest bedroom for visiting family here are some helpful items to leave in their room:

- Your Wi-Fi code, both the name of your network and your password - written down and more than one copy.

- Set of house keys with any security code written down.
- Spare plugs and adapters. If you are pretty sure you own what they will need, let your family know in advance so they don't have to pack their own plugs.
- A collection of snacks and liquids in case jet lag causes them to be hungry or thirsty in the middle of the night.
- Spare local public transport swipe card/s with money loaded.
- Notepad and pen.
- Local attraction brochures.
- Light reading/magazine or whatever might be of interest to your guests.
- Hairdryer.
- Mirror - I am always amazed when bedrooms don't have a mirror.
- Reading lights on both sides. Did you know that reading lights contribute to upgrading a hotel room from three stars to four?
- Clear surfaces. As much as you like the knick-knacks normally residing in the guest bedroom, you are best to clear them away - other than maybe small dishes for rings and jewellery. 'Putting room' is always appreciated.

Expectations

There is wisdom in having realistic expectations during home visits.

There is a part of us that dwells in fantasy believing our children *love* being home and desire to spend all their time with us doing happy, happy families. They *are* pleased to be home and *will* do happy, happy families for half a day, but they want more and that's only natural.

Just as your distance son or daughter tend to take the lead on what's happening when you visit them, likely the same will occur when they visit you. They will have plans which have them out and about, likely in your car. Some visiting families are happy to let you know when they'll be in and when they'll be out, while others tend to keep information closer to their chest. It can be frustrating when you are trying to be host with the most and wish to plan meals and the like.

This is your golden opportunity to cook for your family but you'll probably find it turns into a continuous production line. I always do some cook-ups before family arrive. A big lasagne in the freezer along with a casserole or two will never go amiss. If your family want to cook some of the time, step back, allow them to contribute. If you find it hard to have someone else in your kitchen, once again it's time to, as our children would say, 'take a chill pill'. Instead, take the kids to the park and enjoy the luxury that's maybe rare to you of walking into your home and smelling dinner cooking. Lastly, if they don't clean up or put things where they should be - it can all be sorted later.

Likewise, be prepared for loads of laundry, wet towels left on the bathroom floor and unmade beds. Sometimes grandparents can forget these 'joys' between visits.

Visiting sons and daughters are normally keen to take advantage of all babysitting opportunities so you can expect to have a child or two at home all to yourself on occasions. It pays to think ahead and have a few toys hidden and ideas up your sleeves to entertain little ones. I have found that you don't have to be too creative. Just open the pot drawer, potter in the garden or cuddle up on the couch with a book. I remember a session of pea shelling kept a highchair-bound toddler amused for ages.

And don't forget baking with Grandma, fishing with Grandad or just kicking a ball in the backyard or park. Keep things simple.

Older children need their space. Keeping up with friends back home via devices will remain a priority and they'll fit you in, between everything that is important to them.

It is all too easy for the days to pass and all you seem to do is cook, clean and tidy up. But that's what having the family to stay is all about. In between is laughter, silly moments, surprise cuddles, quiet words, wine infused meal times and the unexpected savouring of silence when they are all out.

Take loads of photos, making sure you are in them also. They are the makings of a terrific memory photo book you can later design, order and post them. The grandchildren will remember their visit so much better when this book keeps surfacing in their toy collection.

VISITS: WE GO THERE

"Distance may be an adversary when family ties
are tight. It can be an ally when they're loose. Time
between visits can settle irritations and ill feelings [...]
You can get along with - endure? - almost anyone if
your time with them has a clear end in sight [...] Above
all, day or night, be on your very best behavior. Be
pleasant, helpful, easy going. Keep opinions to yourself
unless asked. Don't dwell on any drama back home. In
other words, be as likeable as you can be. The warm
afterglow will stretch across visits."
Dr Ray Guarendi, *Being a Grandparent*

Travel is a universal conversation topic for Distance Grandparents who choose to travel and are still able to visit. Frequent flyer programmes, favourite airlines, airline lounges, convenient routes, seating preferences, homeopathic jet lag tablets, noise-cancelling headphones, travel insurance and Economy versus Premium Economy versus Business Class debates litter conversations. Airlines could benefit by a greater awareness of this loyal customer base who likely fly on the same routes, with the same airline, in probably the same seats, never accruing sufficient frequent flyer miles to make them shine as a sales statistic.

As a first-time Distance Grandparent visitor it is natural to assume your family will welcome you into their home with open arms and treat you like royalty. Let's face it, you have paid the airfares, done the miles and arrived with presents. However, a royal welcome is not guaranteed. Your distance son or daughter and family have their own needs and actually, so do you.

Where to Stay?

The question of where to stay has many considerations. Each visit might be different. The things to weigh up are the:

- Length of stay
- Sleeping arrangements on offer at your son's or daughter's home
- Age of the grandchildren
- Strain on existing facilities
- Relationship with the distance middle generation
- Ease of adapting to your new surroundings
- Financial restraints
- Ease of getting around, especially if your preferred choice is off-site

I enjoyed the humorous storytelling of one of Baldassar et al.'s Dutch research participants in *Families Caring Across Borders,* who compared discussions of staying with family to fish in the refrigerator. "Three days is fine, but a couple of weeks does not work."

Your distance family may have the space to host you and that's wonderful. However, there are two good reasons why this might not be ideal.

First, the middle generation may secretly *not* want you to stay, but don't have the heart to tell you. In some situations, one half of the distance couple wants you to stay and the other doesn't. Authors offer amusing observations here.

"What if one parent insists you stay, and the other stays mute, or searches the internet for all accommodation options within twenty-five miles? Unless both are of one voice, accept the hotel printout. The grandkids may vote for your staying, but they're not yet voting age."
Dr Ray Guarendi, *Being a Grandparent*

"Good low maintenance visitors, confronted with cramped sleeping conditions, have been known to spend several nights in a nearby hotel or take off in a hire car for a few days mid-break to explore other parts of the country. Much as your hosts love you and you love them this cuts both ways. It gives your hosts a chance to get their breath back. You could offer to take your grandchildren with you. High maintenance visitors find unfamiliar situations hard to cope with and might be more difficult to please."
Peter Gosling and Anne Huscroft, *How To Be A Global Grandparent*

The second reason it may not work to stay with your family is because you prefer your own space. This is an issue for my husband and me. We are used to 'just us' and need to recreate a quiet home away from home, for an hour or two a day.

Karen (N.Z./England) recounted with philosophical acceptance the blow-up mattress in the lounge, surrounded by drying laundry, that was her space during a solo visit to London - and she managed. It would never have worked if her husband had accompanied her. They would have needed to stay elsewhere.

> *"Like many other grandparents, I renew my energy
> supply from rest and quiet. Making sure that I got
> some every day was critical for my mental and physical
> health on the trip. As much as we love them, having
> to pay constant attention to our grandchildren can be
> exhausting and grandparents are entitled to replenish
> resources, and make some time for themselves."*
> Selma Wassermann, *The Long Distance Grandmother*

A transition decision point often occurs once a second grandchild arrives and space in the family home is at a premium. This was raised by Maureen (N.Z./East Coast U.S.A.) when their second distance grandchild was expected. She felt that she and her husband would likely need to stay somewhere close by as the family home would be at capacity.

Airbnb

Airbnb has become a lifeline for Distance Grandparents preferring their own space. This platform offers ordinarily hard-to-find accommodation in non-touristic suburbs and neighbourhoods. Of course, it comes at a cost and if your distance son or daughter lives in a touristy location, the price increases. In the next chapter I will discuss money and the inevitable weighing up we all do as to what we *want* to pay for, what we *can* pay for and *how long* we might be able to keep doing so.

On my last visit to Atlanta, I managed to reserve an Airbnb that was literally over the back fence from Lucy's condo. Our grandsons could visit, and it became a second home. We were neighbours and this made for an incredibly convenient winter's stay, additionally avoiding the expense of an Uber to and fro.

To drive, or not to drive?

There is no arguing that distance sons and daughters appreciate independent visitors who enable them to get on with their normal routine. Being prepared to drive during visits is a huge plus.

In New Zealand we drive on the left, so we've happily hired cars in the U.K. - but Europe and America is another deal. I *have* ventured out on the other side of the road but I've got to a stage in life where this is a thrill I'm no longer prepared to tackle. If this is you, the next step is to embrace public transport and the likes of Uber. We don't hesitate to figure out bus and train systems and sometimes our grandkids join us on these outings. I rarely use Uber in New Zealand but have become a dab hand at car sharing apps in other countries. We Uber to and from shopping centres, supermarkets, airports and between our Airbnb and family. What's more, overall it's cheaper than a rental car. Next to Airbnb, Uber is the next best friend of travelling Distance Grandparents.

Tact and Diplomacy

Visits call for special reserves of tact and diplomacy. Sometimes learning curves are involved:

"I am an authoritative person. I have no difficulty taking charge - in fact, I prefer doing so. I like organizing events and delegating authority. Many years ago and long before grandchildren were on the horizon, when I made my first visit to my daughter's own home, I had no sooner put my suitcase down than I began to organize lunch. Without a thought for her feelings, I took charge

> in my daughter's kitchen and gave everyone a job,
> efficiently dispatching and delegating. I cringe when
> I think of it. It hadn't taken me but a few moments to
> usurp my daughter's role as mistress of her own home.
> After all, I was the mother. She was my child. Isn't this
> what mothers should do? [...] Having learned to be a
> "driver" it is difficult to play the role of "passenger".'"
>
> "At the very opposite end of grandparents who 'endure
> in silence' are some with excessive expectations. Their
> insistent demands to be looked after, to have things
> their own way, to be entertained, to turn everything
> around to their own satisfaction, will throw the entire
> household into an uproar. Instead of welcoming them,
> children and grandchildren will long for their departure,
> so that life can return to normal."
> Selma Wassermann, *The Long Distance Grandmother*

Veteran Distance Grandparents admit that visits can be littered with highs and lows and that sometimes you're not even sure what the temperature is from day to day. There are magical moments when you have those long-awaited first hugs in the airport's Arrival Hall and later on when a curious grandchild plucks up the courage to gingerly knock on your bedroom door for a morning cuddle. Sometimes grandparents drag themselves around the world and wonder if it was all worthwhile, especially when grandchildren are little and nap times, drawn out meals and scratchy bedtimes dominate each day. Extensive outings are limited, you spend a lot of time at home, children can be out of sorts and oftentimes you can honestly feel like a nuisance.

In Peter Gosling's and Anne Huscroft's publication *How to be a Global Grandparent* there is a chapter titled, 'Are you a Low or High Maintenance Visitor?' These words spoke volumes and made me chuckle. I would also add... 'or Even Welcome at All?', as this can sometimes be the case.

Visits are joy-filled and energising while also emotionally exhausting and challenging. You can't wait to get there... but when it's time to leave, most of the time, you have had enough and you're ready for home. Give and take is required by all parties. When either generation is oblivious to the needs of the other, visits can be strained. When visits work, they are fantastic. When they don't work out, visits can be very stressful and you have to dig deep. What a kaleidoscopic, emotionally draining undertaking!

In *Emotions and Being There* I spoke of travel assignments with a primary purpose to babysit the grandkids. When addressing regular visits, it would be fair to say Distance Grandparents don't want to spend every waking moment with their grandchildren. They want to help but don't want to be seen as on-demand babysitters, even if the distance son or daughter would secretly love them to be that... and perhaps might feel they *should* be. Furthermore, when they all gather socially with friends, the Distance Grandparents don't want to be constantly left in charge of supervising the kids. Distance Grandparents like to have some time to socialise also.

"The very thing that makes the visit special is also what makes it difficult."
Baldassar et al., *Families Caring Across Borders*

Familiarity

I relate to Edward Bruner in *Culture on Tour,* when he explains that there are two ethnographies (scientific description of peoples and culture) of travel. One is the 'performance' of the destination (where our family live and where the familiarity grows with each visit: the nooks and crannies of their neighbourhoods) and second is the 'travelling unit' (you) and those we meet along the way (family, new friends and neighbours we revisit each time).

When you revisit the same destination on a regular basis, the 'performance' and your 'travelling unit' begin to merge into their own site of 'cultural production': a familiar home, way from home. This eases the burden of regularly visiting distance family.

Visits to all our children's cities are packaged with a large dose of ordinariness. We know the aisles of the local supermarkets. We're conversant with the public transport systems and acquainted with the local eateries. We enjoy catching up with neighbours and socializing with our children's friends. I have performed the role of Mother's Help at daycare and as soon as I walked in on a later visit, the teachers and children immediately recognised me. My husband and I even became a familiar enough fixture at a church and were once approached to perform a duty during the service. They thought we were locals.

Lynley (N.Z./England) commented in a happy-go-lucky, confident tone how familiar her journeying has become: same route, same routines, predictable outcomes. "I am comfortable and familiar heading into Heathrow now," Lynley said. "I get on the [Heathrow] Express [train], and I go into the city, and then I get a taxi. Going to London to see the family is a piece of cake [laughing]. It is easy... it is familiar... I know what I am doing."

Sharing worlds

Experiencing the world of your distance family allows you to take your relationship with them to another level thanks to your new-found knowledge of their situation, willingness to immerse yourself in their world and being game for new experiences.

207

There are tremendous benefits for all if the distance and visiting family share their worlds.

"A mind that is stretched by a new experience can never go back to its old dimensions."
Oliver Wendell Holmes, physician, poet, professor and author

Sidetracking briefly, a rarely talked about downside to sharing worlds is how disconcerting it can be for Distance Grandparents to witness how close local friends have become for their son or daughter. They fill the void of the day-to-day absence of immediate family. Making friends as a migrant or expat is not easy but these friends are crucial to feeling embedded in a community and feeling part of a tribe. They are also essential as emergency backups in the way in-country family are at home. Distance Grandparents know intelligently that these warm relationships are invaluable, but emotionally it can be a little confronting, as mentioned earlier in discussions of surrogate relationships, to realise that some aspects of your role have been replaced by someone you hardly know.

However, visits remain an adventure and over the years I have hung out in the expat bubble world, met up in kiddie-focused holiday spots and settled in for a time in fully-immersed, picket-fenced neighbourhood settings.

I can recall a special weekend in London with our university-aged granddaughter. She recommended an Asian fusion restaurant in Covent Garden we would never have picked if we had seen it listed in a guide. I can only describe the incredible lighting, zany décor, interactive technology and out-there menu as a terrific, fun experience. I was glad we didn't go for the safe and familiar and were willing to be led by our granddaughter.

> *"I know a couple who recently visited their young
> adult daughter in Washington, D.C., where she was
> living. They asked her to plan their four-day visit
> around whatever she wanted to do and show them D.C.
> through her eyes. After the visit with their daughter
> was over, they admitted they probably wouldn't have
> chosen the restaurants or sites she showed them, but
> they considered the visit a success because they had a
> wonderful time with her and gained great insight into
> her life. Wise parents."*
> Jim Burns, *Doing Life With Your Adult Children*

I have been grateful for the many opportunities to see our families' worlds through their eyes.

I remember the quintessential English summer's day at Windsor Cricket Club with the glorious castle in the background. It was the setting for one of my grandson's matches, supported by deck-chair-seated, picnic-basket-carrying, upper middle-class family supporters.

In Bangkok I was a guest at a large informal Thanksgiving dinner hosted by a local American embassy staff member and family. The setting was an expansive, tropical-pool level of a high-rise apartment complex and the fare included a turkey with all the trimmings - a prized menu item in expat Thailand. A few years later I was invited to a traditional Thanksgiving dinner on American soil - a beautifully set table, the best crockery and cutlery. Most countries outside of America do not celebrate Thanksgiving. All the more reason it was a privilege to be invited.

In November 2017 we had an extraordinary week in Chicago. On the first day, while heading to our river cruise, we were swallowed up in the estimated five million crowd of supporters congregating for the Chicago Cub's street parade recognising their World Series win after a drought of 103 years.

The next day we attended an iconic rugby match at Soldier Field between the Irish and our world famous All Blacks. We witnessed history when New Zealand lost but this was offset by the joyous, jubilant Irish fans who were so gracious in victory.

One day later, I fumbled with family friction, grief and tears as the Trump election results crossed the television screen in our Airbnb.

And the next morning we went on a pre-booked architectural tour to - of all places - the Chicago Trump Tower hotel, and later the same day I found myself unexpectedly moving and shifting in a tide of protesters with cautiously resolute armed police positioned every few yards - impromptu, peaceful, social-media fuelled, anti-Trump Chicago voters letting off steam. These vivid memories returned when I watched the 2020 elections unfold on television.

That visit was topped off with a joint birthday celebration: my own and my son's future mother-in-law. We were born on the same day, in the same year. How could that week ever match an ordinary November week at home?

In a different way, Atlanta and Chicago have delivered me first-hand tension around the Black Lives Matter campaign. I have never experienced violence or riots but have been sensitive to an undercurrent of looks, glances and foreign, unsettling feelings of bias and white privilege. Visits have also exposed me to the normality of guns in American society. I am unaccustomed to gun shops in most neighbourhoods let alone knowing that people I mix with during visits might be carrying a weapon.

This all makes me appreciate that if I didn't have family in these cities, I would never have had these confronting - if humanising - experiences.

Reflecting on the many visits required, Distance Grandparents often say that by the time they fit in these various visits, in either direction, there is little time, inclination or money to go anywhere else. Baldassar et al. found that their participants also bemoaned the fact they never had a proper holiday due to their family travel commitments. In fairness this can also be felt in reverse by the distance middle generation. It is a price we all pay for being distance families.

Crazy, Magical, Memorable Adventures: "Oh, the Places You'll Go" (Dr Seuss)

Those of us who have been fortunate to travel can recall occasions when memories were created which have gone down in history, as moments in time. One of my favourites is a last-minute jaunt to Sydney, Australia (three-hour flight), where I never ventured further than an overnight stay at an airport hotel.

Lucy was bringing eight-month-old Peter down to New Zealand from Bangkok. This journey involved an overnight flight to Sydney, an early morning transit and a connecting flight to Auckland. A few days ahead I decided to travel to Sydney and surprise Lucy so I could give her a hand on the final leg. I booked on the same return Emirates flight from Sydney to Auckland and thought I had done well securing a seat in the row behind her. (Thanks to the Emirates call centre agent who divulged Lucy's seat number.)

After an uneventful flight over and a quiet night alone at the hotel, I strolled back to the terminal with my carry-on bag and checked in for my return Sydney to Auckland flight, only to find I had been allocated a different seat! Once again, Emirates came to the party. I don't know how the attendant managed it but I was now allocated a seat next to Lucy and Peter in the bulkhead row.

Then began the fun. Once I passed through security, I figured out which direction Lucy and Peter would arrive from. My detective activity paid off and right on cue I was able to stand back from a line of weary, transiting travellers who were placing their hand luggage on a conveyor belt. I saw Lucy in the line with bubs in a front pack. I didn't need to hide. She had her hands full and was plenty distracted. By this stage Peter had to be unstrapped from the trusty front pack and Lucy had all manner of paraphernalia to load on and off the conveyor belt. With Peter on one hip, she gathered all her belongings with the other hand and literally dumped them a short distance away all in a pile on the floor.

As Lucy was crouching over her things, re-strapping Peter in and gathering her belongings, I came up from behind and tapped her on the shoulder. "Would you like a hand?" I asked. What a scream of delight and disbelief. We'll never forget the moment.

If you ever get an opportunity to pull off a crazy, magical, memorable adventure I can heartily recommend it.

Ethical Considerations of Flight Travel

None of us can escape issues of global warming and our obligation to protect our planet. Lynley (N.Z./England) has strong views on the environment and protecting the planet. "It is interesting you get to the stage in life and you do start thinking about how you will be remembered [laughs]," Lynley said. "So, I have a little goal for my grandson. I need him to get involved in environmental science issues and... save the world."

It was a few weeks after our chat that youth climate protest marches were staged in many cities of the world. Swedish teenage climate activist Greta Thunberg grabbed headlines with her passionate cries to world leaders. A new phenomenon dubbed 'flight shaming' was one of her messages, as explained in Mariana Lenharo's article in *elemental*: Greta refused to travel on planes and encouraged others to do the same. Sweden has trail-blazed the campaign with flight shaming a translation of *flygskam*.

In a later conversation Lynley said her eco-conscious, English son-in-law challenged her on this issue, questioning her flights to London. She had to admit she would not reduce her travel; seeing her grandson was non-negotiable.

This situation leaves me pondering. Will there come a time when Distance Grandparents are shamed for boarding a plane to visit their family?

Going Nowhere

Counter to the discussion of *Visits: We Go There...* is the reality of what is being missed by those who cannot or choose not to travel... and how they adjust to that reality.

Peter Gosling continued visiting his family, travelling to Malaysia up to the ripe old age of 87. Don't we all hope our mind, bodies and finances will match or better Peter's record and, also, that our family will let us? It takes an adventurous and caring spirit from *both* sides to execute such undertakings. My husband is older than me. Right now he is fit and able but I wonder what travel will look like in years to come. Will I be juggling a Zimmer frame and packing incontinence pads?

> "We go as often as we can now, while we are able, fit enough to take these flights. We have funds at the moment that we can do so and then there will reach a point it becomes just too hard physically, and/or financially to do so and we will probably just want to do more road trips around New Zealand - maybe the odd trip to the Pacific Islands or Australia for a sun break... but to actually make the huge trip to the States, the East Coast of the United States, is extremely... it's a long way to go."
>
> (Maureen, N.Z./East Coast U.S.A.)

In the past, South Africans Walter and Sandra have visited their family in Australia and the U.S.A. but now feel it won't happen again because of their age. "The tiring inconvenience of long hours' travelling, high expense and the draconic Australian visa requirement [U.S.A. is much easier] takes its toll," Walter said.

Rhonda's and Colin's (N.Z./Germany) brief exchange about their choice to no longer fly is likewise philosophical and accepting.

Me: When was the last time you went to Europe?
Rhonda: 2012... and we won't go again.
Me: It gets harder and harder?
Rhonda: [looking to Colin] Yes. You can't cope with that?
Colin: I can't cope with a flight like that.
Me: It's all just too hard?
Rhonda: Yes.

Shona (N.Z./Scotland), who is still able to travel but copes with her strained distance family situation, reflected on these issues: "The sad thing is when you get old or sick you can't go... because it is too far so what happens to that relationship then? If it [relationship] is strong I guess they would come out and see you... a bit tenuous, but it just doesn't happen. But they [grandkids] are there forever in our hearts and they've turned out, under the circumstances, amazingly good kids. We are proud of that."

Baldassar et al. in *Families Caring Across Borders* reported that when their Irish-based research participants felt unable to undertake further journeys to Australia, they preferred to contribute to fares for their grandchildren and children to visit Ireland. Likewise, as travel insurance becomes more expensive with ageing, there can be financial sense, if funds allow, in this reverse way of handling things. In some ways this is a win-win for all.

Maureen (N.Z./East Coast U.S.A.) went on to sum up well the resilience required around future travel plans: "Sometimes I think *gosh this is hard. This is just hard.* It takes effort and you have got to keep working at it and you know this situation will never change. It is never going to get any better or easier in terms of seeing or having time with them or communicating with them. It is probably going to get harder as time goes on as they have more children and you know... the reality of them coming to New Zealand is going to be very expensive as they will be paying full fares for all their kids to come over and all that sort of thing. I am thinking it is going to get tough as it goes on... And there might be times when... and I have noticed with other families... maybe they have got three kids... and only one kid comes out with a parent."

All Distance Grandparents wrestle with the knowledge that there could come a time when they can no longer travel. Financial restraints, illness or plain old age are the main reasons they transition from being visitors, to being visited. I console myself with an observation that when Distance Grandparents make the decision, it's just one of *many* ageing-related decisions they are making. In some ways it can be a relief.

Travel Advice

How to make Economy a little more fab

As a general rule we travel Economy class and, more latterly, Premium Economy when it is on offer. We have experienced Business Class and First Class thanks to a past life in the travel industry, upgrades with frequent flyer points and just plain good luck, but Economy is the norm.

The ex-travel agent part of my being continuously asks myself, *how can I make Economy better?* Here are my tried and tested, ex-travel agent, frequent flyer suggestions on how to improve Economy.

Noise-cancelling headphones
Buy a set (each) of noise-cancelling headphones. These differ from regular headphones as they perform two functions. First, they replace the plastic headphones airlines supply and give you much better sound. You plug them in like you would the airline headphones and they come with the necessary connections. Second, and importantly, they block out a substantial amount of the background aircraft drone noise. It is not until you remove your headphones during a flight, to say go to the restroom, that you are reminded of how much noise we are normally subjected to.

And don't forget, if you simply want to go to sleep and not watch a movie you can still have them switched on, but not plugged in.

When you go shopping for a pair you will find prices vary from reasonable to a sizable investment. Additionally, you will have the choice of small air buds, in-ear headphones or traditional headphones with large, padded ear sections. I recommend the padded headphones for comfort and functionality. A mid-range price one should do the trick. Some are battery operated (batteries last for a long time) and more recent models are rechargeable using a USB connection. Either is fine.

A side benefit of owning noise-cancelling headphones is you can of course use them when you return home such as on a noisy, daily commute on public transport or reading while someone else has the television on. You do not need to spend top dollar to achieve the goal unless of course you are a real techy in which case only the best will do. Lastly, for the hesitant, they are not complicated to use.

Seating choice

Spend good time working on your aircraft seat numbers. We all know that *where* you end up seated can make an immense difference to your general comfort. There are many factors you have no control over - but there are some you do. Take ownership of your seat numbers, even if you have booked through a travel agent. Some airlines allow you to choose seats at the time of booking, while for others it can only be done closer to the departure time.

There are some basics to remember. Seats near the bulkhead may involve infant noise. Exit seats, of course, offer more legroom but all your gear has to be stowed in the overhead locker for take-off and landing and your screens have to be folded away.

That means you miss movie watching at the beginning and end. Window seats afford you a view, but only when you are beneath the clouds and it's daytime. They also have another downside as you have to climb over other passengers. Also, do a little research on radiation levels in aircraft, especially close to windows.

Our choice is always in the middle section, with one seat on the aisle. Our other choice, if it's offered, are the two seats by themselves (two-sy) directly behind the last row of three, right at the back of the aircraft. They are generally set a little away from the window and give you an extra feeling of space. We have also sat upstairs in Economy in an Air France A380 in a two-sy and it felt like Business Class. The premium positions, like the ones I have mentioned, always go early and there is frequently a charge. Just pay the money - from my experience the cost is worth it.

Even if your travel agent has booked your flights you can generally go online yourself, check the seats they have selected and change them if preferred. If your flights involve different sectors on different airlines you'll need to visit each airline's website to secure the seats. Hint: when visiting the websites of the other airlines, the booking reference for your overall ticket will not work on these sites. Check the small print for the other airline's flight and somewhere that airline's booking reference, just for that sector, will be noted.

My final thought here is: have you ever struck a metal box inconveniently installed near your feet? This media box robs you of valuable space for you and your bags. A great way to check the chance of being blessed with one is to consult www.seatguru. com. You'll need to know the aircraft type for each sector and especially take note of which airline if it is a code-share flight. For those with the patience and desire, time spent dotting every i and crossing every t will be so worthwhile.

Lounges

One of the benefits of Business Class is access to lounges. We all love lounges! As you walk through the door, showing your boarding pass, it's like the gates of heaven have been opened to you. If you are travelling Economy and have a layover, investigate whether the airport has a lounge unaffiliated to an airline, which you can pre-book or just turn up and pay for. Yes, it seems a lot of money to hang out somewhere for a couple of hours, but airport food is expensive and generally very unhealthy. If you can manage to have a healthy snack or meal, decent coffee, top up your water, enjoy some peace and quiet and even freshen up or have a shower you have got your money's worth. If your children are looking for present ideas, you can always suggest airport lounge access for the next visit.

Cabin luggage

First check the cabin bag size allowance for each airline. Wheelie cabin bags are the preferred choice for many. However, we only use those for short, no check-in luggage journeys. For long trips, with checked-in luggage, we have a backpack each - like an oversized school bag with pockets and a place for everything. Additionally, I have a compact, across-the-body handbag for essential items like key documents and my mobile phone.

Backpacks offer many advantages. Once on your back, your hands are free and it's even possible to go to the restroom still wearing it. You aren't anxious about boarding early and finding space overhead for your bag. A backpack can be more easily stowed, if you choose, under the seat in front which means you have access to whatever you need during the flight and don't need to continuously open and close the overhead compartment. If you are getting older and shrinking this becomes a nuisance. Finally, if you are walking down cobblestone lanes with your suitcase, you will be pleased you don't also have a small wheeler cabin bag.

When you start shopping pay attention to the cubic measurement. Ours are 28-litre capacity. That's as large as you want to go. Lastly, a backpack with a second support strap across the middle of your chest is very helpful for your back. Invest in a quality bag.

Sometimes our backpacks have serviced us well for overnight side-journeys. We've managed to squeeze in all we need when the rest of our luggage is being shipped to the next destination.

Suggestions for your 'liquids bag':

- **Nasal drops designed for flights**
  Research shows that keeping your nasal canals moist attracts fewer germs. We each have a spray with our name marked on the bottom, so we know whose is whose. Hint: When you put your sprays in your 'liquids bag' also include a small pack of tissues. You will need tissues when you use the spray and you'll be pleased they are handy!
- **Eye drops**
- **Lip balm**
- **Moisturiser/hand cream**
- **Mask/s**
- **Toothbrush and small toothpaste**

Other non-negotiable cabin gear:

- **Melatonin and/or natural sleep supplements**
  We have tried sleeping tablets but have decided we don't want them in our system as they tend to keep us awake once we arrive. Even take a sleepy/chamomile tea bag if that works for you. Magnesium is also helpful and it is generally recommended to be taken at night. If I want to get some sleep (of sorts) on an overnight flight I will probably take a melatonin, a natural sleep supplement and a magnesium tablet - all three. Of course, the sleep isn't

great, but it is generally enough to get me through, before I see a proper bed.

- **Eye shade to aid sleep**
- **Hay fever/antihistamine tablets**
  Airline travel can bring on hay fever even if you never experience it at home. They are another non-addictive sleep aid.
- **Hand sanitiser**
- **Wipes**
  Handy for the tray table and any unfortunate spillages.
- **Pashmina**
  This is the first thing I wrap around me when I board and it stays on for the whole flight.
- **Padded neck pillow for night time flights only**
  Personally I feel they take up too much space for daytime flights. We'd prefer to include a book.
- **Compression stockings**
  I choose to use them. Yes, they are uncomfortable, but better to be safe than sorry.
- **Empty water bottle**
  You can fill for free, hopefully from a water fountain, after you have passed security. You need to drink more water than is offered by the airline. Of course, not everyone is comfortable using public water fountains.
- **Socks**
  Now you can take your shoes off. I wear the socks over my stockings.
- **Cheap slip-on slippers**
  You'll appreciate them if you visit the restroom and the floor isn't dry.
- **All medications**
  Sometimes airlines lose luggage.
- **All devices and charging gear**
  Just in case there is a flight delay or some other complication. Whatever happens, you need to keep in touch.

Travelling during a pandemic

"[...] in a situation where all flyers are wearing masks, the risk of virus transmission is minimal, even if the airplane is at full seating capacity."
Mariana Lenhoro, citing research by Sean Kinahan, Senior Threat Scientist at the National Strategic Research Institute of the University of Nebraska

Cautionary advice regarding travelling on aeroplanes is inconsistent. Debate rages as to how easily viral transmission occurs within the confines of the cabin and while transiting through airports. In the past we have all caught germs while travelling; however, did it ever occur to us to wear a mask, even when we were well? Previously, only Asian travellers routinely adopted this regime and interestingly many nations from that part of the world reported low COVID-19 infections.

There was a time it never bothered us to see a cyclist ride along without a helmet: these days we would immediately flinch. Travelling on aeroplanes (and trains and buses) has changed for us all. What was normal, is now unacceptable... to most people.

To travel or not to travel... now, or into the future? That is the question. Here is the expert advice from the International Association for Medical Assistance to Travellers (IAMAT):

- Check IATA's interactive map to find out about current global travel, pre-testing, quarantine and isolation regulations (see *Resources*).
- Be prepared for things to go wrong anywhere along the way (changed or cancelled flights or you contract a virus just prior to departure or while away). How well would you cope physically, emotionally and financially?

- Be aware of negative attitudes to international travellers. Even if you are travelling 'home' the door may not be open wide for you.
- Keep up standard influenza shots.
- Don't travel if you are feeling sick or have been in contact with someone who is sick.
- During the flight wipe down the seat, tray table and armrest with disinfectant wipes and keep sanitizer handy, not packed away.
- Wear a face mask, even when sleeping and only remove it to eat or drink.
- Don't eat when others near you are eating. Wait until they have finished and put their masks on again.
- Go to the restroom when there is no queue and, of course, wash your hands thoroughly before returning to your seat.

These resources are updated under the heading of *Travel Advice* at: www.DistanceFamilies.com/resources.

UNCERTAINTY

"Those of us who are ageing in a transnational context, either due to our own migration or that of others, need to organise our everyday lives in a setting that is not limited to a single nation state."
Mobility scholars, Horn et al. cited by Näre, Walsh and Baldassar, *Identities*

Nothing is certain in this world and ageing definitely doesn't come with a paint-by-numbers plan. Distance Grandparents naturally prefer their children to be around when they are frail and less able. Depending on whether this will be their reality or not, ageing can generate foreboding feelings. All Distance Grandparents dwell on the future's uncertainty. It is an ever-present subject, cloaked with a muted veil of apprehension and obscured by an upbeat demeanour. All my interviewees had ponderings for which answers do not exist - around aloneness, money, wellness, travel or no travel, care and support - all the while knowing some or all of their family is scattered.

Lynley (N.Z./England) spoke about the future: "It is pushing me to make other decisions. One of them is if I carry on working. It's putting a dividing line between me and the kids." She spoke about her ideas of living part of the year in London, maybe house swapping. We joked (half-seriously) about the concept of her buying an apartment in London, close to her family, and converting it to an Airbnb for when she was not in residence.

Social Phenomena

As we all live longer, new social phenomena along with cultural and social norms appear, each adding their own slant to ageing and questions of migration's push and pull. Some of these create uncertainty for Distance Grandparents.

The sandwich generation

The concept of the *sandwich generation* can affect any grandparent (distance or otherwise), but when applying the sandwich generation phenomenon to Distance Grandparenting it is a reminder of two daunting scenarios.

First, it isn't unusual to find grandparents in their 70s who still have an elderly parent or two in care. At the same time the other half of their sandwich, their local in-country family *and* distance family, are also looking for support. No other generation has experienced this combination of generational *and* geographical responsibility to the same degree this late in life.

Second, if Distance Grandparents have reached their 90s, their distance son or daughter is likely in their 70s (and has now joined the sandwich generation). Importantly for the Distance Grandparent, the 70s distance children might be too old to travel. This doesn't bear thinking about.

(Physical) Kinlessness

If children aren't around, parents are on their own and need to adjust their plans accordingly. 'Kinlessness', also known as 'elder orphans', is emerging as a contemporary issue and is the terminology scholars use. Their explanations for this phenomenon include fertility (smaller family sizes), death of a spouse and estranged families - and I would add globalisation.

Ken (N.Z./England) told a story of an elderly man he met while visiting his optometrist. The gentleman had been told to bring a support person. It took some convincing before the optometrist understood that the gentleman had *no one* to accompany him because all his children lived in Australia.

Both Hannah's (England/Switzerland and U.S.A.) children live overseas and in recent times she has been widowed. "It was hard. The house was empty... you don't know how to occupy yourself. It takes a lot of time to adapt and accept it. You have to accept it. Most important is to keep communication open."

Society's kinless are often vulnerable and hard to identify, and their personal situations can change without anyone really noticing. Distance Grandparents aren't always obvious in society either and uncertainty can easily be masked. They've had a reputation for being independent and resourceful in the past and they don't want that to change. Distance Grandparents, who a few years ago were regularly jetting here and there, are now less able and could be struggling to ask for help.

Nationalistic norms

In *Visits* I spoke of the cultural attitudes to the concept of (Western) Distance Grandparenting family visits. Here I supply three, albeit extreme, nationalistic migration examples so you can appreciate the vastly different angles of the *push* and *pull* argument and how it manifests into pressure, anxiety and uncertainty within society and families. These examples highlight the vastly different Distance Grandparent situations that occur in our world and are food for thought.

The Philippines

Filipinos do not feature in my book; however, the nature of emigration in the Philippines is a unique case and shines a completely different light on global mobility and uncertainty. The Filipino government actively encourages its citizens to leave its shores and work in other countries, temporarily or permanently. Money earned and sent back home provides a significant boost to the nation's economy, so it makes fiscal sense to support emigration. Parents, couples and children separated by oceans are an acceptable and encouraged norm in the Filipino society. Therefore, uncertainty still exists but comes cloaked in widespread, cultural push factors.

New Zealand

I wouldn't describe New Zealanders as resentful of our departing young. We are, however, mindful of the price the country pays for the brain drain: well-educated citizens taking their expertise overseas. Oftentimes they'll say 'I need to go overseas to expand my career' or 'New Zealand is too small for me'. Sociologist Paul Spoonley, in *The New New Zealand*, acknowledges that these migrants represent a 'significant economic power' and talks of their 'abandonment of the homeland'. This is harsh language but from the Distance Parents' and Grandparents' perspective there remains an unspoken element of truth. All the while, however, like Margaret Mahy said in *Unpacking Distance Grandparents*, we remain proud of their achievements and philosophical, all at the same time. The 'pull' factor of New Zealanders leaving their home country creates uncertainty for those left behind while simultaneously being a well-accepted social norm that just needs to be lived with.

South Africa

South Africa, where emigration is prolific, warrants special attention from the perspective of the left-behind Distance Parents and Distance Grandparents and their resulting kinlessness and uncertainty. The number of Distance Grandparents is high and it's common for all of their children to have left the country. The impact of emigration and kinlessness has become a significant social problem.

South African Clinical Psychologist Maria Marchetti-Mercer, from the University of Johannesburg, is a specialist in emigration. She explains in a *Family Process* article that the impact is 'extensive' and 'multi-folded' in South Africa. What's more, frequently the departing family has been so busy organising their move they have spent little time preparing their folks for life without them. She goes on to explain the consequences: "Emigration is mostly experienced as a vast loss, almost akin to a death, bringing about significant changes in social networks." Furthermore, to leave South Africa is considered to be abandoning the family and nation, both of which are of paramount cultural and moral importance, particularly for Afrikaners.

Australian author and distance South African daughter Hendrika Jooste is well-versed in the field of immigration. In a conversation with me she explained the departed family is frequently ex-communicated by the siblings who remain behind and the subsequent resentment hinders future family relationships. New Zealand Anthropologist Kris Finlayson, who studies the Afrikaner diaspora in New Zealand, goes as far as stating in his master's thesis that a fair percentage of South African emigrants are considered 'traitors to the Afrikaner cause' of helping to fix the country.

Oftentimes the distance son or daughter suggest down the track that their South African parent or parents join them in their new country; however, few take up the offer, as the thought of moving is overwhelming. South Africa, as a home of Distance

Parents and Grandparents, is a particularly concerning nation. Uncertainty and physical kinlessness for South African Distance Grandparents is off the scale.

Kinlessness unfolds before me

When I conducted my university research none of my research participants was kinless. All had either a spouse and/or at least one in-country child.

Sadly when I was buried deep in my thesis writing, I received unexpected news that Jim (N.Z./England), while getting ready for a day on the golf course, had suffered a fatal heart attack. Clive and I were shocked and upset. I had known Jim for 36 years. His wife, Rebecca, has a sister handy but in terms of her immediate family, she became physically kinless overnight. They were my only research grandparents with no children living in New Zealand. This upset me as Rebecca is a soft, delicate person, and I could not imagine her alone. During a phone call she told Clive, "Jim was my rock. He took care of everything."

I witnessed first-hand the theoretical notion of kinlessness become a reality. Her England-based son immediately travelled home, leaving his mother's cherished granddaughter and her daughter-in-law back in the U.K. and he stayed for a few months. A later decision has the U.K. family moving permanently back to New Zealand and as I write this chapter they are currently en route. Fortunately, Rebecca will no longer be a Distance Grandmother and the *Frozen*-themed bedroom will be occupied again. Little did Jim and Rebecca realise when they decorated that room, what a hideaway retreat this will be for their granddaughter as she adjusts to living back on the other side of the world.

About the same time as Jim's passing, Brian and Shona (N.Z./ Scotland) had their worlds ripped apart when Brian was diagnosed with a terminal condition. Months of treatments followed and during the writing of this book I lost another friend and fellow Distance Grandparent. Shona now navigates her strained distance family situation as a Single Distance Grandparent. Connections are just that bit tougher now she doesn't have Brian by her side. Fortunately, her strong in-country family remains a steadfast support.

Death: digital preparation

As we age we all know the importance of keeping our will up to date and ensuring our affairs are in some sense of order. As we find ourselves attending more funerals as friends and family pass, thoughts and preferences around our own funeral begin to form. Perhaps we'll relay this to our in-country family as they're close by. It's easier to bring the subject up face-to-face than with distance family when we're conscious that connection time with them is precious.

When you are dead and gone it could be very stressful for your in-country family to explain your funeral preferences to your distance family. The distance sibling may question the validity of the instructions and want to do things a different way. You may have taken some time to settle on your funeral preferences, maybe even chopped and changed your ideas along the way. Your distance family hasn't been privy to that thought process.

One solution is to create a digital vault of instructions. This could be as simple as a cloud-based shared folder in the likes of Google Drive or similar. Note your wishes, load the document online and give your family access to the file. It could even be a continuous 'work in progress'. For example, you might start with the basics of your funeral and go on to write your own eulogy, note your preferred funeral hymns - even write the service! There will be no doubt about what is expected. Your in-country family will be grateful they don't have to make all the decisions (and relay those decisions) and your distance family can focus on travelling home or coping with their grief from afar. Your family will be forever grateful for your efforts.

The Big Unknown

Talk of ageing populations, sandwich generations, kinlessness, new society norms, digitally recorded funeral instructions and no in-country family all leads to the question of The Big Unknown. We all wonder:

- How will life look down the track for Distance Parents and Grandparents?
- How should Distance Parents and Grandparents prepare for the future?
- What should the distance family be considering in this equation?
- What services will need to be out-sourced?
- Will the money be there to pay for them?

The classic findings of British Sociologists Dame Janet Finch and Professor Jennifer Mason state that family responsibilities are not straightforward. They are the result of 'longstanding processes of negotiation based on a combination of normative guidelines and negotiated commitments' (cited in Baldassar et al., *Families Caring Across Borders*). Distance Grandparents feel it is their responsibility to take care of themselves as best they can, for as long as they can manage, while quietly hoping, when they *truly* need a family member, someone will be there for them.

The Conundrum of Money

Money makes the world go round - and money definitely makes Distance Grandparenting go round.

Driving Forces

What are the driving forces, from a grandparent's perspective, tussling for attention when navigating the small everyday expenses of life and the big-decision commitments of Distance Grandparenting?

Pride and independence

Baby Boomer Distance Parents tend to be very independently minded. It's a matter of pride that we pay our own way. When visiting distance family, grandparents, myself included, want to contribute our share - that's a given and discussed in more detail shortly. This comes from a desire to set a good example and not to be a burden. We doggedly *want* to take care of ourselves in our old age, with or without children handy. But is this realistic?

A desire to support your children evenly

As a family grows, parents normally try not to favour one child over the another, whether it be through time, money or attention. This is an honourable strategy but when Distance Grandparenthood arrives nothing much remains even in your family. When one child maybe lives five minutes away and the other is 5,000 miles away your even strategy hits a snag. This becomes a dilemma for Distance Grandparents. You're outlaying large sums to visit family overseas while the local family rarely sees that level of expenditure on them, all the while knowing *they* will need to be there for their parents when more support is required down the track. All sides of the discussion, will from time to time, feel like a knotty tug of entanglement.

Lending money

The *Bank of Mum/Mom and Dad* is a contemporary term whereby parents offer and/or provide financial support to their adult children. Nowadays it is an economic force to be reckoned with as the Baby Boomers head to retirement. Journalist Naaman Zhou reported in *The Guardian* that if Australian parents combined were a bank, they would be the ninth-largest home loan lender in the country - more significant than the Bank of Queensland. Pressures can be placed on the Bank of Mum/Mom and Dad from all quarters. Some are welcome, some are not.

Will my savings expire before I expire?

It is a fact that Distance Grandparents are wealthier than previous generations; however, they are also living much longer, so whatever we've accrued needs to see us through to the end. It is a concern when savings aren't high, and like the proverbial phrase, 'how long is a piece of string?' A juggling act takes hold in your brain continuously assessing how much is in the bank, how long it will need to last and what services and help you will need to pay for seeing as your family is scattered.

Changing attitudes

In *Key Findings: The How It Is,* and throughout this book, the discovery that *Change is a Constant Companion* is often mentioned. What you saw as your responsibilities 10 years ago could be quite different now. Thoughts and attitudes regarding money shift and change all the time, whether it is about what you spend on your family or how you spend money on yourself. For example, you may have always shunned Business Class, claiming, "There's nothing wrong with being down the back." Then one day, to heck with it, you have had enough and up the front you go. I've been there.

Nationalist values

Even within English-speaking Western nations, values and expectations vary as family financial support is expected, requested or needed *of* grandparents and in reverse... expected, requested or needed *by* the grandparents, from the distance middle generation.

Who pays for what during visits?

Who pays for expenses during visits, in either direction, is subjective and a lot of factors are at play. No one wants to sit at home for every meal and we all want to get out and visit places together.

Should expenses be the exclusive responsibility of the higher earner or the one with greater discretionary income? Distance Grandparents may know, for example, that their son's or daughter's family is struggling financially. Picking up the tab is a way to support and give the family a treat. Or maybe if one has paid for the airfares the other is responsible for expenses while you are all together? There are no hard and fast rules.

Let's assume your financial situations are somewhat similar. Below are some suggestions for when *you* visit and hopefully these shared expenditure patterns will be duplicated when *your family* visit *you*. The most important aspect is consistency, so your family know where they stand during each visit.

- Pay for your own accommodation, especially if you want control of the standard, location and facilities.
- Pay for what is important to *you*, for example the costs associated with alone time activities with individual family members.
- Pay every second supermarket visit.

- Pay for every second fill at the petrol station.
- Pay for some meals out but hold back sometimes and allow the local family to pay.
- If you have discussed in advance that you'll visit certain attractions, arrive with pre-purchased tickets for some, but not all.

On the flip-side here is an example where we didn't follow my own advice and decisions evolved organically with no fuss. Most times when we visit our U.K. family, we holiday together somewhere. We started sharing a chalet or apartment but as the grandchildren grew older (and we grew older as well) we progressed to two separate units. There has been no hard and fast rule about how the accommodation account is settled. Sometimes we have split the bill, sometimes we have paid the lot and other times our distance family has paid. The latter doesn't sit right with us but on the other hand, we have done the travelling, invested in the airfares and need to allow them the opportunity to contribute in that way. They also get to choose where we go!

Some readers may baulk at my suggestions or even be offended. You might feel differently. Money is a tricky subject at the best of times. What I am sharing is what has worked for our distance family visits. You need to decide what sits right with you, what you can afford and gives you peace of mind.

Twilight years: you pays your money and you takes your choice

How aware are social services and senior care facilities of Distance Grandparents, scattered families and the social phenomenon of kinlessness? Is there a belief that the flourishing industry of retirement villages, with attached care wings, will take care of this growing population? Furthermore, have retirement villages considered including in their business model furnished apartments that might be rented short-term by residents' visiting family? How progressive would that be?

In *Families Caring Across Borders*, Baldassar et al. highlight that governmental policies have a significant impact on distance familying practices of care. They state, for example, that New Zealand authorities, compared to many other nations, accept a greater degree of obligation to care for their older citizens. I for one, even as a privileged New Zealander, would not want to rely solely on the state.

Whether Distance Parents have family handy or not, they will likely find themselves purchasing care services so they can retain their independence. This is referred to as the commodification of elder care. If there is *no* family nearby, then the transition will likely commence *earlier*. This could start with paying for a house cleaner, to moving into a lifestyle retirement village or employing a live-in carer. One certainty of *The Big Unknown* is that pay-as-you-go caregiving services will likely be an ingredient of Distance Grandparents' senior years.

When I socialise with my Distance Grandparent friends and the subject of money comes up, I jokingly discourage their Bank of Mum/Mom and Dad activities from being overly generous. I remind them, with a sheepish grin, "Don't give too much away. When we are old and need to get to the doctor or supermarket it might be Driving Miss Daisy transporting us." (Driving Miss Daisy is a New Zealand companion driving service aimed at the older or less able. It is a player in a growing market of senior services.) And what about launching Uber for Seniors - for the digitally able? These conversations tend to generate responses of thoughtful deliberation from my friends as they ponder the uncertainty of a future unknown.

The upside of the likes of Driving Miss Daisy and other such services is they are an avenue for distance sons and daughters to arrange and/or contribute funds - for others to do what they are unable to do. There is nothing ideal about this arrangement but it is proactive familying and has its place.

I include this commentary about money as it contributes to my argument that Distance Grandparenting sits on uneven terrain. Absence, presence, loneliness and worry all have a home in a discourse about old age and potential kinlessness. All seniors contemplate their future when one or more of their children live a long way overseas and they know their backup support systems aren't as robust as they could be.

> **“ All seniors contemplate their future when one or more of their children live a long way overseas and they know their backup support systems aren't as robust as they could be. ”**

A precious promise

The conversation below on the topic of money and old age particularly impacted me.

Me: I remember you once said Stuart [distance son] stated, "There will always be money for an airfare."
Rhonda (N.Z./Germany): Yes, that's right and Diane [his wife] said the same thing and the kids here [in-country son and family] said there is always money to go to Ireland [reverse distance familying situation].

What the siblings meant by this is if something is a problem at home in New Zealand (or Ireland) and the parents need them, their distance son (and local son in reverse) will find the money for an airfare (and make the time). These are powerful, gutsy offers delivering bucketloads of calm and peace of mind. They say 'you're so important to us, we'll find a way'. For Distance Grandparents who have reached the age that the body isn't so willing and life is starting to slow down a tad, these assurances lessen uncertainty and are incredibly comforting.

In-country Family: Treat Them Like Gold

Repeatedly I have stated the importance of the in-country family: the siblings who have not moved overseas. When Distance Parents are elderly and need more assistance, devoted in-country family truly shine and are a lifeline to both their parents *and* their distance siblings. A well-functioning distance family is not a two-sided affair. It is three sided and the in-country sibling (or siblings) is the third side of the family triangle: they can reduce uncertainty for all.

I was reminded of this in a conversation with my New Zealand stepdaughter who has been a Community Hospice nurse for 15 years. She's regularly in the homes of the dying, witnessing family after family coping as best they can. In her opinion, it takes an exceptionally well-functioning, supportive family, with *more than* one sibling nearby, to provide the necessary hands-on care to the most frail. Most families, she admits, struggle to cope. Add middle generation children living overseas and this prospect is a concern for all.

Local siblings never asked for their unequal share of responsibilities and sometimes resentment accumulates while caring for ageing parents. Hendrika Jooste (South African distance daughter living in Australia) shared in a conversation with me, examples of in-country South African siblings who booked an out of town holiday to coincide with their brother's or sister's home visit. They exclaimed in the same way a new mum does when her partner walks in the door and she hands him the baby: "They're... all yours."

From a Distance Parent's perspective we need to be quietly vigilant about these peripheral family dynamics. We *are* inadvertently piggy in the middle but it remains our responsibility to never allow our in-country children to feel taken advantage of. It helps if *they* know that *you* know they carry the greater parental support burden and you're grateful for their presence.

My advice to distance sons and daughters from the first day a decision is made to emigrate or work temporarily or permanently overseas, is to treat your in-country family like gold. They can have a huge impact on how Distance Grandparenting *is* for the Distance Parents and, furthermore, how it *is* being a distance son or daughter. In *Being a Distance Son or Daughter - a Book for ALL Generations* I will write about coping with sick and dying parents at a distance. This, without a doubt, is the toughest gig of being a distance son or daughter.

Final Reflections: Uncertainty

Some topics around Distance Grandparenting are clean cut and obvious and others, like those in this chapter, are not.

Ivan's (N.Z./East Coast U.S.A.) quiet and deliberate summation about uncertainty has a valuable message: "There is a time when I know we might get sick and then we'd like to think they [distance family] might come out and that's when... those decisions have to be made where it is just not practical for the whole family to travel... they see it as important for one to travel... and I accept that... The key is you don't pre-empt what it is all going to look like or how it is going to be. The moment you do that you form a picture in your head, and it takes a bit to get over it. So, the more you can keep it to just every day... keep on the even keel."

'Never say never' is a handy phrase when traversing Distance Grandparent senior years. None of us know what is around the corner and what we might need to embrace (or pay for) even if we'd prefer it wasn't that way.

FINAL BIG-PICTURE QUESTIONS

"The big picture doesn't just come from distance; it also comes from time."
Simon Sinek, author and motivational speaker

In this chapter I stand back and take in the broad picture of Distance Grandparenting with a longitudinal gaze. I ask some questions that don't necessarily have straightforward answers and I do my best to share some wisdom.

How Has the Past Affected the Present?

Psychology Professor Robyn Fivush from Emory University, Atlanta, is known for her research on the parent-child narrative and the development of an autobiographical self. She says in a *Memory Studies* article, "One's own story is embedded in the stories of others in the past and the present." Fivush goes on to say reminiscing helps past events make sense of current issues and places "one's own life in the context of familial history".

Reminiscing is like origami

Surprisingly often, Distance Grandparents reminisced about how they, or their parents, had moved towns, cities and (for some) countries during their lifetime. I hadn't anticipated how frequently reminiscing would feature in chats: family history was never on my agenda.

Marco Gemignani, a native of Italy, is an Associate Professor of Psychology at the Universidad Loyola Andalucía in Seville, Spain, and shares the analogy in a *Qualitative Inquiry* article of origami as a way of explaining reminiscing. His findings complement those of Robyn Fivush. He describes his research participants' reminiscing as a process of folding and unfolding, creating context and order to their thinking. Gemignani points out that just as an origami can be unfolded and the paper used again, pasts are continually being 'rewritten, told, silenced, and forgotten'.

The interview process for my Distance Grandparents research prompted ponderings like the folding and unfolding of origami. For some, grandparents reminiscing is a reminder, or realisation, that Distance Grandparenting has been nothing new within their family circle.

Ken and Nancy (N.Z./England) immigrated to New Zealand from England with a 10-month-old decades ago. They admit they gave little thought to how their respective parents in the home country had felt when their family continued to grow on the other side of the world.

Similarly, three of the grandparents were coincidentally raised in the same North Island town, a good six hours' drive from Auckland, and moved north as young adults. They all commented that in those days the distance between the two cities was a lifetime away and reflected on how it must have been for their own parents.

"If we go back to the family from afar, in my case I moved [north]. It was a long way in those days. When you put it in context, it is not much different from what we are doing now [travelling to England]. In fact, it was probably harder because they [his parents] couldn't afford to travel up and down the country and there was no FaceTime. They probably had a harder time than we do... Taking it one step further we never felt we were doing any injustice to our parents."

Jim (N.Z./England)

Karen (N.Z./England) reminisced about her reverse Distance Parent relationship: "Well, I think from my perspective, when I had my children my parents were in Australia, we had Distance Grandparenting then. So initially, for the first three years, it was good. We saw them at least twice a year, or we'd go over there. But I remember Nicole being 14 months old before Mum and Dad actually saw her, and that was a pity."

Lynley (N.Z./England) has researched her genealogy and this has caused her to reflect even more on her family history and her current situation: "I guess working on the family tree has made me think about the journey a lot of my family have done and my grandfather... came to New Zealand [from England] in 1927. What they did was amazing. My grandmother was the youngest of 13. She left behind all of her brothers and sisters."

Lynley indicated, more than once, that our interview had made her think. "In fact," she said, "sitting here talking to you clarifies my thinking a little bit more about what's happening out there."

Reminiscing helps Distance Grandparents to balance their thoughts and accept their role in scattered family situations.

How to Mend Fences

"Communication is the true measure of any relationship."
Gransnet.com

This statement is correct but communication for Distance Parents and Grandparents comes with strings attached. What might work when families live down the road, doesn't necessarily work across the world.

Niggly issues

Niggly issues, small misunderstandings and cultural confusions are, despite not necessarily being *conflict*, best addressed fast. This is the stuff of everyday life and most times easily solved with a genuine 'sorry' even if you honestly think you aren't to blame. It is a case of going the extra mile, digging deep and accepting that distance creates confusion and upset. Being prepared to not always being right is helpful.

Issues greater than those on the niggly scale are sadly challenging to solve at a distance. Oftentimes situations can crop up well exceeding the parameters of 'there are two sides to every story'.

Disagreements and differences of opinion that can't easily be brushed aside

These are the sorts of issues that if you lived close you would make time to talk things through. Timing would be important. You might, for example, ensure small children weren't around. Maybe a dinner is arranged and a bottle of wine opened. Likely it could take a few attempts for the situation and timing to be just right.

Trying to do all this by distance is nigh on impossible, so for most Distance Grandparents the problem ends up in the too hard basket and, given time, you simply move on. Psychologists and Empathy scholars Lidewij Niezink and Katherine Train talk of this strategy as 'Suspending Assumptions Practice'. This is 'the art of noticing, recognizing, and naming' our evaluation of emotions, thoughts and events and allowing these experiences, in time, to 'pass through you'. In other words, time and distance will diffuse the sting, allowing acceptance in some form or other to find a home.

Serious conflict

True conflict and polarised views are rarely solved with even the most genuine heart-to-heart conversation. Sometimes one party isn't even prepared to acknowledge there is a problem. An attempt to solve conflict may involve interfering in the marriage or partnership of their distance son or daughter and most would view this as no-go territory.

"At any age, people drawn into a rift become immersed in the painful emotions of others, through no fault of their own."
Karl Pillemer, Family Sociologist and Professor of Human Development, *Fault Lines*

If there is a glimmer of hope, the less-difficult distance son, son-in-law, daughter or daughter-in-law is contactable separately and you are able to explain your concerns one-on-one, then you have a responsibility to at least try. This is an example where it pays to have multiple communication mediums in your communication arsenal as encouraged in *Communication Routines*, so you can easily touch base.

Outside of that option I would say:

- Serious conflict is rarely solved via digital platforms.
- Serious conflict is rarely solved during a fortnight visit.
- Maybe, with dedication from both sides, conflict *might* be unravelled a *little*, during a long summer break together, ideally in tandem with professional counselling... but you can't start dialoguing the night before returning home.

There is an old saying that 'hurting people hurt people'. This is the root cause of much family conflict. Addictions, past trauma, co-dependent relationships, a need for control, insecurities, emotional baggage and inappropriate interference are all potential ingredients of the experienced hurt which, when not understood, can cause someone to hurt others in turn.

"When people try to function in areas that affect their untended wounds and unhealed hurts, they inevitably hurt others. Often they wound others as severely as they were hurt, and in remarkably similar ways. While most hurting is relatively mild, deeply wounded people deeply wound others."
Sandra D. Wilson, Family therapist and author of *Hurt People Hurt People: Hope and Healing for Yourself and Your Relationships*

Books can help. There are suggested titles in *Resources*. Learn about these conditions. Your new-found knowledge won't necessarily right the wrongs but it will confirm *you* aren't the problem and maybe there isn't any solution.

The other advice, as mentioned in *Emotions, Bad News and Crises*, is for Distance Grandparents to receive professional counselling. Learning to live with serious distance conflict requires the input of professionals. This book is insufficient.

Is There an Ideal Default Setting for Distance Grandparenting?

"Play is a 'love currency' that makes a deposit into your children's lives no matter what their age."
Jim Burns, *Doing Life With Your Adult Children*

There isn't a Distance Grandparenting guidebook that doesn't mention the importance of playfulness and infusing fun and laughter into Distance Grandparenting. For some personalities this is a normal modus operandi. For others, including myself, it is not instinctive.

"Nowhere is it written that grey hair and bifocals mean the end of a playful spirit, of comic invention, or of a giving up of a sense of the absurd... Step only between the cracks in the pavement, talk to flowers, wear a funny hat and sip soda through a curly straw - have fun with your grandchildren."
Selma Wassermann, *The Long Distance Grandmother*

I am the first to encourage a grandchild to sit with me on the sofa and I'll read them a book, but I am slow to gravitate to the floor and enjoy mayhem and mess. And please don't ask me to go on the highest slide at the water park. However, when I do stretch myself, act the fool and be a little stupid the grandchildren love it and, what's more, it makes their parents hoot with laughter too.

On a Christmas visit I followed this advice and we once arrived with cheap, silly Santa hats and plastic party glasses. They cost next to nothing, didn't last long, but we had a few laughs. We even wore them to the pub on Christmas Eve. We would never do that at home.

Back home we once hosted a FaceTime red party with our smaller distance grandsons. We dressed from top to toe in red and gathered red food and red items from around the house to share and talk about. On standby for added attention were red themed YouTube videos queued on an iPad and displayed to them via the camera.

None of this comes naturally to Clive and me. Fun activities take some thought and preparation, but the little ones love them and it's what they remember.

Are There Benefits to Distance Grandparenting?

"We have been able to experience different cultures and taken great pleasure in seeing our grandchildren grow up in a variety of environments. The greatest benefit has been watching the boys become true citizens of the world."
Peter Gosling, *Grandparenting from long-distance*

Since a fair proportion of my discourse has focused on the less encouraging aspects of how Distance Grandparenting *is*, it seems only honest and appropriate to say, from my own perspective and others, there *are* plenty of positives, especially if one takes the attitude that one door opens and another closes.

Rosemary and Barry (N.Z./England), for example, are happy about transnational familying as mentioned in *Emotions and Loss, Acceptance and Resilience.* They thoroughly embrace it and love the freedom Distance Grandparenting gives them.

The pluses

Here are the pluses from my perspective:

- **No babysitting**

  At home, I observe some of my grandparent friends who appear continuously tired and worn out from minding their grandchildren and seem unable to navigate a healthy balance to this obligation. I recall a local grandmother friend who (in a particularly low, out of character, fed up, feeling-used moment) told me, "You're lucky your grandchildren live overseas."

- **A tidy house**

  Little ones make mess. I am not a minimalistic, fanatical housekeeper but I do enjoy living in a generally tidy, reasonably clean house.

- **Car seat free**

  I must confess to enjoying the luxury of not having child car seats permanently installed in our cars, accompanied by the inevitable flux when they need to be removed or re-installed. It's nice to know there are no squashed raisins buried in the upholstery, stains from spilled drinks or sticky-finger residue anywhere. While writing this chapter we have traded in Clive's 14-year-old second-hand car for our first-ever, brand-new and shiny one. If we had little grandchildren handy you can be sure no car seats would be allowed to grace *this* new motor - and *my* car would become the default messy little-people transporter!

- **Travel**

  I like to travel and I know I am not alone. Subject to time

and finances, grandparents are able to tag on interesting stopovers and fun side excursions when they visit family. I have followed umpteen posts on Facebook of intoxicating travels by Distance Grandparents and I am known for my appealing posts and photos. Many of these travels would not have taken place had it not been for the need to visit family. I am grateful for all these many adventures.

- **Time**
  I have time for me and time for my husband. I still need to schedule time for digital catch-ups and fortunately all our family is happy to book these in advance. So generally I know what is happening, and when. Outside of that my leisure time is my own, to fill as I choose: I write my own schedule/diary/calendar.

- **Hobbies and interests**
  There is more time for hobbies and outside interests and you don't feel guilty about doing something for yourself or others. I am on committees and have time, brain space and the energy to contribute to community initiatives.

- **Digital competency**
  The need to connect with family digitally demands an acceptance and embracing of technology and a willingness to upgrade and reboot my competency and skills. This improves many aspects of our day-to-day lives.

- **Global thinking**
  Globalisation requires me to embrace diversity and different cultures. I cannot live in my own middle-class white pocket. Adaptability, emotional resilience, constant give and take are day-to-day strengths going hand-in-hand with global familying and there is no let-up. This all keeps me young at heart, which bodes well for maintaining vibrant connections with all generations.

Satisfaction

I admit it never occurred to me to ask Distance Grandparents, or myself, how *satisfied* we each were with our grandparenting role - distance or otherwise. However, I acknowledge it is a question that is occasionally raised by researchers.

From my perspective it is totally appropriate to consider how satisfying your *marriage* is, as this is a union you were involved in forming and have some control over. Distance familying is a dynamic that is beyond our control and the best way to maintain healthy relationships is to accept and make the most of it, rather than making judgements on a scale of 1 to 10. There is a saying I know I overuse but it seems to fit the bill: 'It is... what it is'.

Purpose - freedom for reinvention

For most of us, work and family life have dominated much of our 'doing' of life. As we approach our senior years, work tends to become less of a focus (if at all) and family is now scattered. This can affect our sense of purpose and identity. Distance Grandparents benefit by becoming aware of this transition and it can be good.

Parenting and Family Researcher Kira M. Newman in the *Greater Good Magazine* wrote of Author and Intergenerational Advocate Marc Freedman, who explains: "[...] few of us wake up one day with a totally new purpose in life." Instead, he observes people draw on the skills, knowledge and values they've cultivated over a lifetime to start a new chapter.

Where would my life have gone, what direction would it have taken if I hadn't been a Distance Grandparent? My undergraduate degree, my master's journey, perhaps this book series may not have happened if I had needed, more latterly, to manage regular in-country grandparent duties. These pursuits have contributed to my current purpose in life and also my identity.

Distance Grandparents, I can recommend finding a new purpose if you are feeling a little adrift.

What is the Difference Between *Distance* and *Distant* Grandparenting?

June Terry (N.Z./Australia), a fellow grandmother and Anthropology master's colleague, has a distance daughter and family in Perth, Western Australia. Naturally she didn't escape my questioning. My colleague generously shared an intimate story that shone a contrasting light on the questions of *what is distance?* and *how far is far?*

Distance is assumed to be geographical; however, there are other forms of distance.

In 1988, June's eldest daughter fell pregnant when she was fourteen. The mother was European Pākehā and the young father was Māori (indigenous New Zealander). The baby was legally adopted to a childless couple on the father's side of his family. This baby was my colleague's first grandchild. The open adoption was the right decision decades ago and the now thirty-something is a happy, thriving woman with strong Māori heritage and identity.

However, a sad void remains for June. Over the years, June has occasionally visited her granddaughter and these days there are connections with several family members via Facebook. She explained to me, with a sadness in her voice, how she has been hesitant to impose her 'white Pākehā-ness' on her granddaughter and cause any upset.

When I asked what the greater distance was - her daughter and other grandchildren in Perth (7½ hour expensive flight and a four-hour time zone difference), or a three-hour drive down the road to her first-born grandchild and a cultural divide - my colleague said the latter.

Distant grandparenting is real too.

"I Am Still Grieving. How Do I Move On?"

Distance Grandparenting is like a challenging jigsaw. The picture on the box looks daunting and you would rather put the puzzle back in the cupboard. Once the edge is done the remaining pieces still don't look like they will ever make a finished picture but with time and perseverance each piece finds its place in the same way a routine of Distance Grandparenting begins to emerge for you. But please, PLEASE don't knock the table.

But maybe you're still saying to yourself, *I have read your book, absorbed everything you have had to say. I understand acceptance is the key... but I still feel pretty sad.*

My final word comes from Melissa Parks, an American Clinical and Health Psychologist who supports the globally mobile. She writes of the difference between self-compassion and self-pity.

"There's a big misconception that being kind to ourselves is the same as feeling sorry for ourselves, which is why I want to clarify the difference between self-compassion and self-pity [...] Self-pity tends to say "poor me," self-compassion recognizes that life is hard for everyone. It allows us to feel less isolated when we're going through a hard time [...] I also want to clarify that self-compassion doesn't mean invalidating how we're feeling. Your pain is still important and deserving of validation and soothing. We don't just push the hard moments 'under the rug.' However, we also don't want to get overidentified with our emotional experience and caught up in the story. Instead, we acknowledge what we're feeling with kindness and that tends to help us process and let go [...] more quickly."
Melissa Parks, www.intentionalexpat.com

If your distance family situation is here to stay, make self-compassion your most loyal buddy.

❝ If your distance family situation is here to stay, make self-compassion your most loyal buddy. ❞

The End

January 2021

I have come to the end of my formal chapters. This book writing project has been a blast - harder than I thought but rewarding in ways I never imagined.

My intention has been to give Distance Grandparents a voice. I asked them how Distance Grandparenting is for them and I've shared their answers.

Distance Grandparents and Distance Parents are a varied bunch and our circumstances differ. However, I hope there are topics you have related to and that I have brought to life... your version of *Being a Distance Grandparent*.

I salute the distance sons, daughters and grandchildren who have taken the time to read this book. As mentioned on the back cover, learning about distance familying from your parent's and grandparent's perspective is an act of love. I hope you have experienced some new understandings and increased your empathy for the folks back home... because that has always been my No. 1 goal.

Thank you for supporting this distance families project.

Helen Ellis
Founder
DistanceFamilies.com

P.S. This is not quite the end. Turn the page for *A Last Word: Viral Uncertainty*

A LAST WORD: VIRAL UNCERTAINTY

"One of the concepts which scare the modern human, is the idea of being unaware of what is going to happen next. Because we're so used to following trends, science, research and predicting what will happen next, we become shocked when an anomaly presents itself."
Roshan Bhondekar,
Indian-born Spanish author, columnist and film-maker

My daughter, Lucy, works at Centers for Disease Control and Prevention (CDC) based in Atlanta, Georgia, U.S.A. In January 2020 she mentioned in a text that she might be seconded to a special taskforce to oversee an escalating virus called COVID-19. At the time I gave the message little consideration - "What virus?"

A lot has changed since then.

"In the past few months, life around the globe has changed beyond recognition as an invisible and deadly enemy has forced us all into varying degrees of lockdown. The dramatic changes to our daily lives caused by the COVID-19 pandemic happened so fast that we didn't have much time to contemplate the effect it would have on us, leaving us feeling shaken, afraid, and disorientated."
Carole Hallet Mobbs, Expat Life Mentor, ExpatChild

Stories from the COVID Trenches

Let's revisit some of the grandparents you have come to know through these pages. What was happening mid-March 2020 when borders closed and their worlds catapulted into an abyss of Distance Grandparenting uncertainty?

For sixteen precious days Rhonda and Colin (N.Z./Germany) and their in-country family delighted in the presence of their oldest grandchild from Europe. Her visit was unexpectedly cut short by two weeks when it became scarily obvious she should return home immediately. Flight options were limited and airline communications precarious. Late one evening Rhonda emailed me. Her granddaughter had managed to board a flight from Auckland with just 10 minutes to spare. "By the end of the drama all I could do was cry," she wrote. I know how much they love their granddaughter. They worry about her welfare and felt short changed.

Lynley (N.Z./England) said, "The kids are coming early [excitedly]. They're on a flight from Heathrow tonight. It's like they're escaping the country. They have voluntarily isolated themselves for the last week or so and brought forward their visit before the borders might close. I will move in with friends around the corner and they can have my house for two weeks to self-isolate. They're bringing their laptops and can work remotely. Maybe they might think it is pretty good here and decide to stay."

When Lynley phoned I was buried in paperwork cancelling our upcoming U.S.A. family visit. We were due to leave in 10 days' time. It was our first visit in 14 months and my reward for the year I had taken off from travel to complete my master's. I was pleased for Lynley that in the middle of the disturbing mire of daily bad news and the continuous recalibrating of our thinking, there was a good news story.

Several months later I can report that Lynley's family are still in the country. They have found a place to rent, retained their U.K. jobs and are getting up in the middle of the night for Zoom work meetings. Future plans remain up in the air.

In another file on my desk were flight bookings we'd made in January 2020 for Lucy and our U.S. grandsons to visit New Zealand for two weeks during Christmas 2020. Another visit that was later cancelled.

I kept asking myself, and I still do... *How long will it be before I can hug my children and grandchildren?*

> **" How long will it be before I can hug my children and grandchildren? "**

Maureen and Ivan (N.Z./East Coast U.S.) were also booked to visit America and Maureen exclaimed, "All our [travel] plans, [have] turned to custard... and we have yet to meet Grant [new baby grandson]. I spoke to Nigel [distance son] this morning and couldn't hold back tears... because he's also thinking his business will go under... which makes things so very hard for them too!"

Rosemary, (N.Z./England) has a gentle sense of humour. She emailed me, "It sure is a mess, like surround sound, [you] cannot escape the upset." Consistent with her previous responses, she philosophically admitted she was not hard hit by the virus impact and did not have the emotional attachment to her distance family in the same way she knew I did. I once again admired her level-headed stance.

Change (not again!)

As I review the chapters and topics in this book, every aspect of Distance Grandparenting has been afflicted by the COVID-19 effect. None has sneaked under the radar. In the words of Psychologist, Psychotherapist and Digital Nomad Dr Sonia Jaeger in her personal blog, "For many of us, the 'new normal' is not normal at all [...] The pandemic has turned our world upside down."

Over the months of in and out lockdowns coinciding with the writing of this book, I noticed that Distance Grandparents, who previously were happy to talk about their distance familying experiences, became a tad reticent to open up. They were, and still are, finding life tough. It's hard to speak on the subject. COVID-19 is changing them. They're struggling to keep their emotions intact.

Acceptance (not again!)

Acceptance, once again, is the key to adjusting to life with a pandemic. Just as parents and grandparents need to *accept* their familial roles as Distance Parents and Distance Grandparents, they also need to *accept* the existence of the pandemic.

In *Emotions and Loss, Acceptance and Resilience* I explained *The 3 H's - The language of progressive acceptance* of Distance Grandparenting. Below Dr Jaeger takes Elisabeth Kübler-Ross's famous Five Stages of Grief and relates them to The Language of Pandemic Acceptance.

The Language of Pandemic Acceptance

Stage 1: Denial
"The virus won't affect us. It's a hoax!"

Stage 2: Anger
"My freedom and security is gone. Why are you making me stay home?"

Stage 3: Bargaining
"Will it get better if I social distance for 2 weeks?"

Stage 4: Sadness
"I want all of this to end. It's making me sad."

Stage 5: Acceptance
"This is happening. I have to create a plan on how to move forward."

Currently there is no line in the sand for Distance Grandparenting - no imminent return to normal. In fairness, the best Distance Grandparents can manage is to uncomplainingly languish, albeit temporarily (we hope), at Stage 5. If you have reached there... well done. You deserve a pat on the back.

Distance Grandparent COVID-19 Questions

Continuously swirling around in the minds of Distance Grandparents are the same unanswered questions.

- Will I escape COVID-19 and, if not, what are my chances of surviving it?
- How long will it take for vaccine distribution to be sufficiently successful so international travel will recommence?
- Once this happens will I still be robust and confident enough to tackle distance family visits or will I have lost my travel mojo, or worse still feel too anxious or frail?
- Will travel insurance companies exclude seniors (or everyone) from pandemic medical cover, thus becoming a *gatekeeper* of future travel?
- Will my family *allow* me to travel? During lockdowns *some* seniors have been deluged with well-meaning advice from their children (distance or otherwise) not to go out, not to socialise and to stay home. There has been little space for these parents to decide their own fate: what they feel able to cope with and what is best for their well-being.
- Will my child/children decide to return home and repatriate? As much as I might enjoy this prospect, is it the right decision for them? Will they feel forever cheated they couldn't lead the lifestyle they previously had in place and how easily would they settle at home? My son or daughter might feel somewhat at home in their passport country but will my grandchildren, who are global citizens, find home completely foreign?

The Future - Balancing Risk

Many Rites of Passage have been missed and will continue to be missed. We have accepted we cannot attend our son's June 2021 wedding in Chicago and will need a crash course in hosting a live-streamed event when we host a gathering for their grounded New Zealand family and friends.

Right now, stories of family visits and travelling Distance Grandparents aren't thick on the ground. When I heard that Distance Grandmother Yvonne Quahe (East Coast U.S.A./ England and Switzerland) had found the courage to get on a plane during 2020 and go for it, I had to know more.

"We decided that we would take a risk and fly to visit our kids," Yvonne said. "Initially this decision would involve an investment of 24 days in quarantine outside of our time with family. We flew from Washington, D.C., to London, quarantined for 14 days and then joined our daughter. Once there we didn't do much... just walks and pottering around the local shops. The next stop was Geneva, arriving during a partial lockdown. We were lucky as just prior to our arrival Switzerland removed its 10-day mandatory quarantine requirement. What a blessing - we could go directly to our son, daughter-in-law and grandson. When we first arrived my grandson was slightly puzzled to see and hear familiar voices that he only knew via a phone. Quickly he adjusted. Now I am helping out and babysitting for a few hours here and there."

When I asked Yvonne 'was the risk worth it?' her response was unequivocally 'yes'. I admire Yvonne's pluck jetting away during 2020 and going for it. Now she has returned, like the rest of us, she struggles with the knowledge that she doesn't know when she'll cuddle her grandson again.

Travelling to family, if and when it happens, will be a balancing act of risk in a way it never has been before. I'm grateful for the safety net of my home country but live with some of the strictest border controls. New Zealand Distance Grandparents wonder if we'll ever use our passports again.

Some Certainties

In a recent communication, when addressing a number of academic colleagues, one of my university lecturers, Dr Graeme MacRae, said, "As Anthropologists, we know better than most that 'normal' isn't necessarily normal and 'other worlds are possible'." He went on to talk of Anthropologists' responsibility to contribute to this debate. As a fledging Anthropologist I will do my best.

There *are* a few certainties about whatever our new normal will be:

- We'll be forever affected by COVID-19 and our experiences will impact the way we conduct our lives in the future.
- We'll never take for granted the ability to fly around the world.
- We'll never take for granted future opportunities to physically connect with families.
- Non-changeable, non-refundable airfares will have little appeal and become a dinosaur of the past.
- COVID-19 has been a viral war and wartime experiences build bonds.
- Many existing expats and migrants are seriously considering returning home during the next year or two and for most these plans were never on the drawing board in early 2020.

- Western globalisation and migration is no longer dominated exclusively by pull factors. Push factors are now evident.
- Western globalisation and its ease of mobility has lost its sparkle. Future foreign career assignments to migrate and work overseas will become less common.

It is interesting now to reflect on a statement made back in 1998 by German Anthropologist Christoph Brumann.

"The resilience of kinship in globalization-affected societies and the question whether humanity is gaining or losing in the globalization process calls for further investigation."
Christoph Brumann, *Anthropos*

Have distance families gained or lost as they've scattered themselves around the globe? Right now it's a difficult question to answer.

Hope

While hope is thin on the ground I finish with two reassuring expert messages. The first is from Distinguished Professor Paul Spoonley from Massey University where I studied. As an expert demographer he claims things *will* get back to normal.

"The impacts of COVID-19 on mobility and migration have of course been significant and enormously challenging and disruptive, but normal services will resume, more or less, as the 2020s proceed."
Distinguished Professor Paul Spoonley, *The New New Zealand*

The second message of encouragement comes from the now globally recognised Dr Anthony Fauci, Director of the U.S. National Institute of Allergy and Infectious Diseases (NIAID). During his only Australian interview to date he declared with gutsy resolve how the pandemic would come to an end.

"We're going to get out of this, guaranteed, [...] It's gonna end in Australia. It's gonna end all over the world. Because we have the capability of doing it, and it's up to us."
Dr Anthony Fauci, quoted by Adrianna Zappavigna in the *NZ Herald*

Although statistics will never be published I believe that in January 2020, just before the virus invaded our lives, we had the greatest population of Distance Grandparents ever known. COVID-19 has been a war - a viral war. Wars change values, priorities and the directions of lives. Over the next few years, and as 2020 has shown us, *some* of our distance sons and daughters will decide that a life of mobility or settling in another land is no longer for them. With mixed emotions they will return. Never again, or certainly in our lifetime, will distance families be as commonplace as we have known in the past.

Helen Ellis
January 2021

RESOURCES

These resources are regularly updated at: www.DistanceFamilies.com/resources

The Distance Family Book Series

If this book has piqued your interest in distance families - don't stop. Here are my other two titles, due for publication in 2021/2022:

Being a Distance Son or Daughter - a Book for ALL Generations
Being a Distance Grandchild - a Book for ALL Generations

Distance Grandparenting is just one third of the distance families story. If your goal is to increase your understanding and empathy for the other generations in your family - these books are for you.

Visit www.DistanceFamilies.com for publication details and where to purchase.

Books

The 5 Love Languages by Gary Chapman
Northfield Publishing, 1992
> Chapman has written an extensive range of books focusing on *The 5 Love Languages*. Be sure to check out all his titles.

Opportunities to show your love to your distance family are all too brief. Once you understand the love language principles it will help you appreciate how *you* like to be loved but more importantly how each member of your family likes to be loved. For example, don't waste money sending endless presents to a person who isn't a 'Gifts Love Language' person. To a certain degree presents are wasted on them. In contrast, be sure to give a 'Quality Time Love Language' family member your undivided attention, without distractions, whenever you call. These are easy habits to embrace and incredibly effective. This is one of the most powerful, incredibly useful books I have ever read.

Doing Life with Your Adult Children: Keep Your Mouth Shut & The Welcome Mat Out by Jim Burns
Zondervan, 2019
If you struggle with 'letting go' and supporting your children to head out into the big scary world, this is the book for you. It comes with a strong Christian theme and includes a section about bringing kids back to faith.

Long-Distance Grandparenting by Wayne Rice
Bethany House Publishers, 2019
If you want to nurture the faith of your grandchildren but you can't be there in person, this is the book for you.

Third Culture Kids by David C. Pollock, Ruth E. Van Reken and Michael V. Pollock
Nicholas Brealey Publishing, 3rd edition, 2017
If you have a strong interest in globally mobile families, this is the 'TCK Bible': foundational teachings of growing up multiculturally.

Raising Global Teens by Dr Anisha Abraham
Summertime Publishing, 2020

> Out of touch with your teenage grandchildren? If you would like to explore the hot topics that globally-raised adolescents experience today, this is the book for you.

Misunderstood by Tanya Crossman
Summertime Publishing, 2016

> If you would like to understand how international mobility affects children while they live overseas, when they return and as they mature into adults, this is the book for you.

This Messy Mobile Life by Mariam Navaid Ottimofiore
Springtime Books, 2019

> If your distance family is multicultural, multi-location, multi-language, multi-values and/or multi-faiths, this is the book for you.

Families Caring Across Borders, Migration, Ageing and Transnational Caregiving by Loretta Baldassar, Cora Vellekoop Baldock and Raelene Wilding
Palgrave, 2007

> If you would appreciate delving into a scholarly while still very readable book about how distance families care for each other across the globe, this ethnographic account is for you.

Invisible Grandparenting by Pat Hanson
Park Place Publications, 2013

> If you are sadly estranged from your grandchildren due to personality conflicts, custody issues or consequences of choices made long ago, this is the book for you. Further resources are available at: www.invisiblegrandparent.com

Fault Lines - Fractured Families and How to Mend Them by Karl Pillemer
Avery/Penguin Random House, 2020
> If you have estrangement in your family, I can't recommend this book highly enough. Distance family estrangement could be as basic as a distance son, daughter (or in-law) preferring not to be present during video call catchups. It's tough. This book will help give you some answers.

Stop Walking on Eggshells by Paul T.T. Mason and Randi Kreger
New Harbinger Publications, Inc, 2nd edition, 2010
> If a member of your family continuously dwells on the past, is controlling, appears to have issues with everyone and everything (could even be described as 'toxic') this book will not necessarily solve the problem but will put this person's behaviour into perspective.

Codependent No More by Melody Beattie
Hazelden Publishing, 2nd edition, 1992
> If you often lose yourself in the name of helping and/or changing others with self-destructive behaviour, this book is for you.

Websites

www.DistanceFamilies.com
This website is for this book series

www.distancefamilies.co.za
> This website is dedicated to South African distance families (connected to DistanceFamilies.com)

www.thelongdistancegrandparent.com
Meaningful and simple ways to stay connected across the miles

www.gransnet.com
U.K. based online community for over 50s

Families in Global Transition (www.figt.org)
A globally mobile forum for individuals, families and those working with them.

Facebook

Distance Families: www.facebook.com/DistanceFamilies
The Facebook page for this book series project

Being a Distance Grandparent: www.facebook.com/groups/distancegrandparent
A private Facebook group for Distance Grandparents (connected to DistanceFamilies.com)

Podcast

The Grand Life
Author Emily Morgan hosts an excellent exploration of grandparenting (local and distance), the relationships within the role and the ways in which grandparenting impacts our children... and their children.
www.thegrandlife.libsyn.com

Professional Services

Families in Global Transition - The Counseling and Coaching Affiliate
> A professional subgroup in the FIGT community
> www.figt.org/counseling-coaching-affiliate

For additional professional and counselling services please visit:
www.DistanceFamilies.com/resources

BIBLIOGRAPHY

A FIRST WORD: VIRAL UNCERTAINTY

Book

King, Michael (2001) *Tread Softly*, Cape Catley: Marlborough Sounds, N.Z.

ABOUT THIS BOOK

Books

Ellis, Carolyn (2004) *The Ethnographic I: A Methodological Novel about Autoethnography*, AltaMira Press: Walnut Creek, CA.

Falk, Ursula A. & Falk, Gerhard (2002) *Grandparents: A New Look at the Supporting Generation*, Prometheus Books: Amherst, NY.

MY STORY

Books

Borofsky, Robert (2018) 'Public Anthropology', in Callan (ed.) *The International Encyclopedia of Anthropology*, John Wiley & Sons Ltd: Hoboken, NJ.

Rhoads, Robert A. & Szelényi, Katalin (2011) *Global Citizenship and the University: Advancing Social Life and Relations in an Interdependent World*, Stanford University Press: Stanford, CA.

Articles

Borofsky, R. (2019) 'An Anthropology of Anthropology. Is it time to shift paradigms?', *Centre for a Public Anthropology*, Kailua, HI.

Podcast

Schneider-Bean, Sundae (2020) '179: Distance Grandparenting With Helen Ellis', *Expat Happy Hour*, https://www.sundaebean.com/2020/06/08/179-distance-grandparenting-with-helen-ellis/

THE DISTANCE FAMILY BOOK SERIES - A SNEAK PREVIEW

Books

Abraham, Dr Anisha (2020) *Raising Global Teens,* Summertime Publishing: U.K.

Bormans, Carine & Geukens, Marie (2020) *Expat Partner,* Lannoo Publishing: Leuven, Belgium.

Burns, Jim (2019) *Doing Life with Your Adult Children*, Zondervan: Grand Rapids, MI.

Crossman, Tanya (2016) *Misunderstood - The impact of growing up overseas in the 21st Century*, Summertime Publishing: U.K.

Gosling, Peter & Huscroft, Anne (2009) *How To Be A Global Grandparent,* Zodiac Publishing UK Ltd: Rutland, U.K.

Huo, Meng, Fuentecilla, Jamie L., Birditt, Kira S. & Fingerman, Karen L. (2020) 'Empathy and Close Social Ties in Late Life', *The Journals of Gerontology: Series B,* Vol. 75, iss. 8, pp. 1648-1657.

Janssen, Linda A. (2013) *The Emotionally Resilient Expat*, Summertime Publishing: U.K.

Pollock, D.C., Van Reken, R.E. & Pollock, M. (2017) *Third Culture Kids*, 3rd edn., Nicholas Brealey Publishing: London, U.K.

Conversation
Romanes, Bridget (2020)
https://www.linkedin.com/in/bridget-romanes-a0171922/

UNPACKING GRANDPARENTING AND DISTANCE GRANDPARENTING

Books
Ahmad, Dohra (2019) *The Penguin Book of Migration Literature*, Penguin Books: New York, NY.

Beck, Ulrich & Beck-Gernsheim, Elisabeth (2014) 'The Global Chaos of Love: Towards a Cosmopolitan Turn in the Sociology of Love and Families', in Treas et al. (eds.) *The Wiley Blackwell Companion to the Sociology of Families*, 1st edn., John Wiley & Sons Ltd: Hoboken, NJ.

Carsten, Janet (2004) *After Kinship*, Cambridge University Press: Cambridge, U.K.

Kerslake Hendricks, Anne (2010) *Changing roles: the pleasures and pressure of being a grandparent in New Zealand: A Families Commission report*, Wellington, N.Z.

Mahy, Margaret (2000) 'I'll say this bit', in Else (ed.) *Grand Stands*, Random House: Auckland, N.Z.

Stafford, Laura (2005) *Maintaining Long-Distance and Cross-Residential Relationships,* Lawrence Erlbaum Associates: Mahwah, NJ.

Wassermann, Selma (2001) *The Long Distance Grandmother,* Hartley & Marks Publishers Inc: Vancouver, Canada.

Articles
Banks, Stephen P. (2009) 'Intergenerational ties across borders: Grandparenting narratives by expatriate retirees in Mexico', *Journal of Aging Studies,* Vol. 23, pp. 178-187.

Carsten, J. (2000) 'Introduction: cultures of relatedness', in Carsten (ed.) *Cultures of Relatedness,* Cambridge University Press: Cambridge, U.K.

Eriksen, Thomas Hylland (2010) 'The challenges of anthropology', *International Journal of Pluralism and Economics Education,* Vol. 1, no. 3, pp. 194-202.

Key, Sir John cited in Edmunds, Susan (2020) 'New Zealand vulnerable to cyber attacks, Key says', *Stuff,* https://www.stuff.co.nz/business/300043661/new-zealand-vulnerable-to-cyber-attacks-key-says

Skrbiš, Zlatko (2008) 'Transnational Families: Theorising Migration, Emotions and Belonging', *Journal of Intercultural Studies,* Vol. 29, iss. 3, pp. 231-246.

Waxman, Barbara (2020) 'Covid's ageist reckoning and what you can do about it', *Stanford Centre of Longevity,* http://longevity.stanford.edu/covids-ageist-reckoning-and-what-you-can-do-about-it/

Image

Wikimedia Commons (2012) 'Standard time zones of the world', https://commons.wikimedia.org/w/index.php?curid=22694730

Film

Silvestri, Alan (1991) *Forrest Gump: Original Motion Picture Score*, Sony Music Entertainment: New York, NY.

Conversation

Seidel, Anna (2020) https://www.linkedin.com/in/anna-seidel-expat-coach-trainer-global-mobility/

KEY FINDINGS: THE *HOW IT IS*

Books

Bruner, Edward M. (2005) *Culture on Tour*, University of Chicago Press: Chicago, IL.

Pink, Sarah (2015) *Doing Sensory Ethnography*, 2nd ed., Sage: London, U.K.

Wassermann, Selma (2001) *The Long Distance Grandmother*, Hartley & Marks Publishers Inc: Vancouver, Canada.

COMMUNICATION ROUTINES

Books

Bangerter, Rhoda (2021) *Holding The Fort Abroad*, Summertime Publishing: U.K.

Gribben, Trish & Geddis, David (1991) *Pyjamas Don't Matter*, Playcentre Publications: Auckland, N.Z.

Rice, Wayne (2019) *Long-Distance Grandparenting*, Bethany House Publishers: Bloomington, MI.

Wassermann, Selma (2001) *The Long Distance Grandmother*, Hartley & Marks Publishers Inc: Vancouver, Canada.

Articles
Cao, Xiang (2013) 'Connecting Families across Time Zones', in Neustaedter et al. (eds.) *Connecting Families*, Springer-Verlag: London. U.K.

King-O'Riain, Rebecca Chiyoko (2015) 'Emotional streaming and transconnectivity: Skype and emotion practices in transnational families in Ireland', *Global Networks*, Vol. 15, iss. 2, pp. 256-273.

Madianou, Mirca & Miller, Daniel (2012) 'Polymedia: Towards a new theory of digital media in interpersonal communication', *International Journal of Cultural Studies*, Vol. 16, iss. 2, pp. 169-187.

EMOTIONS AND LOSS, ACCEPTANCE AND RESILIENCE

Books
Baldassar, L., Vellekoop Baldock, C. & Wilding, R. (2007) *Families Caring Across Borders*, Palgrave Macmillan: Basingstoke, U.K.

Blainey, Geoffrey (2001) *The Tyranny of Distance*, Pan Macmillan Australia Pty Ltd: Sydney, Australia.

Coe, Cati (2014) *The Scattered Family*, University of Chicago Press: Chicago, IL.

Field, Tiffany M, (2001) *Touch*, Massachusetts Institute of Technology: Massachusetts, MA.

Gibran, Kahlil (1972) *The Prophet,* Cox & Wyman Ltd: U.K.

Gosling, Peter & Huscroft, Anne (2009) *How To Be A Global Grandparent,* Zodiac Publishing UK Ltd: Rutland, U.K.

Guarendi, Ray (2018) *Being a Grandparent,* Franciscan Media: Cincinnati, OH.

Janssen, Linda A. (2013) *The Emotionally Resilient Expat,* Summertime Publishing: U.K.

McAuliffe, Phil, (n.d.) The Lonely Diplomat, <u>www.thelonelydiplomat.com</u>

Turner, Toko-pa (2017) *Belonging,* Her Own Room Press: Salt Spring Island, British Columbia, Canada.

Vogels, Robyn & Jooste, Hendrika (2020) *Your D.I.Y. Move Guide to Australia,* Your Move Guide: Melbourne, Australia.

Articles

Baldassar, Loretta (2007) 'Transnational Families and the Provision of Moral and Emotional Support: The Relationship between Truth and Distance', *Identities: Global Studies in Culture and Power,* Vol. 14, iss. 4, pp. 385-409.

Boss, Pauline (1980) 'Normative Family Stress: Family Boundary Changes across the Life-Span', *Family Relations,* Vol. 29, no. 4, pp. 445-450.

Boss, Pauline (2007) 'Ambiguous Loss Theory: Challenges for Scholars and Practitioners', *Family Relations,* Vol. 56, Apr 2007, pp. 105-111.

Boss, Pauline (2012) 'The Myth of Closure', *Family Process,* Vol. 51, pp. 456-469.

Boss, Pauline (2016) 'The Context and Process of Theory Development: The Story of Ambiguous Loss', *Journal of Family Theory & Review,* Vol. 8, pp. 269-286.

Byron, Tanya (2020) 'Our son and grandson are in New Zealand and we are in tears over not being able to be with them', *The Times,* https://www.thetimes.co.uk/article/our-son-and-grandson-are-in-new-zealand-and-we-are-in-tears-over-not-being-able-to-be-with-them-8bt7vvqnk

Frers, Lars (2013) 'The matter of absence', *cultural geographies,* Vol. 2, iss. 4, pp. 431-445.

Hsu, Elisabeth (2008) 'The Senses and the Social: An Introduction', *Ethnos,* Vol. 73, iss. 4, pp. 433-443.

Kalish, Nancy (2010) 'Over The River & Through The Woods: Long Distance Grandparenting', *Psychology Today,* https://www.psychologytoday.com/nz/blog/sticky-bonds/201006/over-the-river-through-the-woods-long-distance-grandparenting

Sevier, Holly (2013) 'Distance Grandparenting', in Singh (ed.) *Indian Diaspora: Voices of Grandparents and Grandparenting,* Sense Publishers: Rotterdam, The Netherlands.

Shavin, Dana (2018) 'To Love and to Envy', *Psychology Today,* https://www.psychologytoday.com/nz/articles/201805/love-and-envy

Sigad, Laura I. & Eisikovits, Rivka A. (2013) 'Grandparenting across borders: American grandparents and their Israeli grandchildren in a transnational reality', *Journal of Aging Studies*, Vol. 27, pp. 308-316.

Sinanan, Jolynna, Hjorth, Larissa, Ohashi, Kana & Kato, Fumitoshi (2018) 'Mobile Media Photography and Intergenerational Families', *International Journal of Communication*, Vol. 12, pp. 4106-4122.

Skrbiš, Zlatko (2008) 'Transnational Families: Theorising Migration, Emotions and Belonging', *Journal of Intercultural Studies*, Vol 29, iss. 3, pp. 231-246.

Solheim, Catherine A. & Ballard, Jaimie (2016) 'Ambiguous Loss Due to Separation in Voluntary Transnational Families', *Journal of Family Theory & Review*, Vol. 8, pp. 341-359.

Sparkes, Andrew C. (2009) 'Ethnography and the senses: challenges and possibilities', *Qualitative Research in Sport and Exercise*, Vol. 1, iss. 1, pp. 21-35.

Podcast
Schneider-Bean, Sundae (2020) '179: Distance Grandparenting With Helen Ellis', *Expat Happy Hour*, https://www.sundaebean.com/2020/06/08/179-distance-grandparenting-with-helen-ellis/

EMOTIONS AND RELATIONSHIPS

Books
Burns, Jim (2019) *Doing Life with Your Adult Children*, Zondervan: Grand Rapids, MI.

The New Granny's Survival Guide (2019), Vermilion: London, U.K.

Inkson, Kerr & Thorn, Kaye (2011) 'Flight of the Kiwi', *University of Auckland Business Review,* Vol 14, iss. 1.

McCall Smith, Alexander (2019) *To the Land of Long Lost Friends,* Little Brown: Boston, MA.

Meyer, Erin (2014) *The Culture Map,* Public Affairs: New York, NY.

Ottimofiore, Mariam Navaid (2019) *This Messy Mobile Life,* Springtime Books: U.K.

Wassermann, Selma (2001) *The Long Distance Grandmother,* Hartley & Marks Publishers Inc: Vancouver, Canada.

Articles
Drew, Linda M. & Silverstein, Merril (2007) 'Grandparents' Psychological Well-Being After Loss of Contact With Their Grandchildren', *Journal of Family Psychology,* Vol. 21, iss. 3, pp. 372-379.

Toth, Csaba cited in Micacchioni, Sara (2020) 'Interview with Csaba Toth', *global people transitions.com,* https://globalpeopletransitions.com/interview-with-csaba-toth/

Stage Play
Hall, Roger (2020) *Winding Up.* Sourced 1 March 2020 from: https://www.asbwaterfronttheatre.co.nz/auckland-theatre-company/2020/winding-up/

EMOTIONS AND BEING THERE

Books

Baldassar, L., Vellekoop Baldock, C. & Wilding, R. (2007) *Families Caring Across Borders*, Palgrave Macmillan: Basingstoke, U.K.

Gosling, Peter & Huscroft, Anne (2009) *How To Be A Global Grandparent*, Zodiac Publishing UK Ltd: Rutland, U.K.

Hanson, Pat (2013) *Invisible Grandparenting*, Park Place Publication: Pacific Grove, CA.

Kleinman, Arthur (2014) 'The Search for Wisdom: Why William James Still Matters', in Das et al. (eds.), *The Ground Between*, Duke University Press: Durham, NC.

Hage, Ghassan (2014) 'Eavesdropping on Bourdieu's Philosophers', in Das et al. (eds.) *The Ground Between*, Duke University Press: Durham, NC.

Segalen, Martine (1986) *Historical Anthropology of the Family*, Cambridge University Press: Cambridge, U.K.

Spoonley, Paul (2020) *The New New Zealand*, Massey University Press: Auckland, N.Z.

Teitsort, Janet (1998) *long distance grandma*, Howard Publishing: West Monroe, LA.

Wassermann, Selma (2001) *The Long Distance Grandmother*, Hartley & Marks Publishers Inc: Vancouver, Canada.

Articles
Sevier, Holly (2013) 'Distance Grandparenting', in Singh (ed.) *Indian Diaspora: Voices of Grandparents and Grandparenting*, Sense Publishers: Rotterdam, The Netherlands.

Silver, Marc (2019) 'Lessons From a Long-Distance Grandfather', *nextavenue*, https://www.nextavenue.org/lessons-from-a-long-distance-grandfather/

Conversation
Quahe, Yvonne (2020)
https://www.linkedin.com/in/yvonne-quahe-6083ab32/

EMOTIONS, BAD NEWS AND CRISES

Books
Arber, Sara & Timonen, Virpi (2012) *Contemporary grandparenting: Changing family relationships in global contexts*, The Policy Press: Bristol, U.K.

Behar, Ruth (1996) *The Vulnerable Observer: Anthropology That Breaks Your Heart*, Beacon Press: Boston, MA.

Hanson, Pat (2013) *Invisible Grandparenting*, Park Place Publication: Pacific Grove, CA.

Articles
Jappens, Maaike & Van Bavel, Jan (2016) 'Parental Divorce, Residence Arrangements, and Contact Between Grandchildren and Grandparents', *Journal of Marriage and Family*, Vol.78, pp. 451-467.

Thomas, Ann & Bovington, Lauren (2017) 'Impact of divorce and separation on children', *ExpatChild*, https://expatchild.com/divorce-separation-effect-on-children/

RITUALS AND TRADITIONS

Books
Awdry, Rev. W and Awdry, Christopher (various) *Thomas The Tank Engine (The Railway Series)*, https://en.wikipedia.org/wiki/List_of_books_in_The_Railway_Series

Gilderdale, Betty (2000) *The Little Yellow Digger Stories*, Scholastic New Zealand Ltd: N.Z.

Gosling, Peter & Huscroft, Anne (2009) *How To Be A Global Grandparent*, Zodiac Publishing UK Ltd: Rutland, U.K.

Janssen, Linda A. (2013) *The Emotionally Resilient Expat*, Summertime Publishing: U.K.

Miller, Daniel (2008) *The Comfort of Things*, Polity Press: Cambridge, U.K.

Miller, Daniel (2010) *Stuff*, Polity Press: Cambridge, U.K.

Yelavich, Brando (2018) *Wildboy*, Puffin: N.Z.

Articles
Gardner, Katy & Grillo, Ralph (2002) 'Transnational households and ritual: an overview', *Global Networks*, Vol. 2, iss. 3, pp. 179-190.

Film
Frozen (2013) Walt Disney Pictures.

VISITS

Books
Baldassar, L., Vellekoop Baldock, C. & Wilding, R. (2007) *Families Caring Across Borders*, Palgrave Macmillan: Basingstoke, U.K.

Articles
Földes, Ionuț & Savu, Veronica (2018) 'Family Practices Across Generations and National Borders', Studia UBB Sociologia, Vol. 63, iss. 2, pp. 143-169.

Gebicki, Michael (2019, Apr 30) 'Number of Australians with a passport: Where we travel and why', *Traveller.com*, https://www.traveller.com.au/number-of-australians-with-a-passport-where-we-travel-and-why-h1dxwt

VOA News (2018) 'Record Number of Americans Hold Passports', *VOA News*, https://blogs.voanews.com/all-about-america/2018/01/18/record-number-of-americans-hold-passports/

Website
Wikipedia (n.d.) New Zealand Passports, https://en.wikipedia.org/wiki/New_Zealand_passport

VISITS: THEY VISIT HOME

Podcast
Schneider-Bean, Sundae (2020) '179: Distance Grandparenting With Helen Ellis', *Expat Happy Hour*, https://www.sundaebean.com/2020/06/08/179-distance-grandparenting-with-helen-ellis/

VISITS: WE GO THERE

Books
Baldassar, L., Vellekoop Baldock, C. & Wilding, R. (2007) *Families Caring Across Borders*, Palgrave Macmillan: Basingstoke, U.K.

Bruner, Edward M. (2005) *Culture on Tour*, University of Chicago Press: Chicago, IL.

Burns, Jim (2019) *Doing Life with Your Adult Children*, Zondervan: Grand Rapids, MI.

Guarendi, Ray (2018) *Being a Grandparent*, Franciscan Media: Cincinnati, OH.

Gosling, Peter & Huscroft, Anne (2009) *How To Be A Global Grandparent*, Zodiac Publishing UK Ltd: Rutland, U.K.

Seuss, Dr (1990) *Oh, the Places You'll Go!*, Random House: New York, NY.

Wassermann, Selma (2001) *The Long Distance Grandmother*, Hartley & Marks Publishers Inc: Vancouver, Canada.

Articles
Coffey, Helen (2019, June 5) 'Flygskam: What is the flight-shaming environmental movement that's sweeping Europe?', *The Independent*. Sourced 15 June 2019 from: https://www.independent.co.uk/travel/news-and-advice/flygskam-anti-flying-flight-shaming-sweden-greta-thornberg-environment-air-travel-train-brag-a8945196.html

Lenhoro, Mariana (2020, Nov 19) 'Read This Before You Fly Anywhere for the Holidays', *elemental.medium.com*, https://elemental.medium.com/read-this-before-you-fly-anywhere-for-the-holidays-cff4b03a1831

Websites
Holmes, Oliver Wendell (n.d.) *PassItOn*
https://www.passiton.com/inspirational-quotes/3586-a-mind-that-is-stretched-by-a-new-experience

Seat Guru
www.seatguru.com

UNCERTAINTY

Books
Baldassar, L., Vellekoop Baldock, C. & Wilding, R. (2007) *Families Caring Across Borders*, Palgrave Macmillan: Basingstoke, U.K.

Spoonley, Paul (2020) *The New New Zealand*, Massey University Press: Auckland, N.Z.

Articles
Näre, L., Walsh, K. & Baldassar, L. 'Ageing in transnational contexts: transforming everyday practices and identities in later life', *Identities*, Vol. 24, iss. 5, pp. 515-523.

Marchetti-Mercer, Maria C. (2012) 'Those Easily Forgotten: The Impact of Emigration on Those Left Behind', *Family Process*, Vol. 31, iss. 3.

Marchetti-Mercer, Maria C. (n.d.) LinkedIn
https://www.linkedin.com/in/maria-marchetti-mercer/

Zhou, Naaman (2019, Jun 30) 'What first-homebuyers should know about 'bank of mum and dad'', *The Guardian*, Sourced 22 October 2019 from:
https://www.theguardian.com/australia-news/2019/jul/01/what-first-home-buyers-should-know-about-bank-of-mum-and-dad

Master's thesis
Finlayson, Kris (2018) 'Wie is ek?: a study of Afrikaner identity in New Zealand', Master's Thesis, *Massey University*, Auckland, N.Z. https://mro.massey.ac.nz/handle/10179/15089

Website
Driving Miss Daisy (n.d.). Sourced from:
www.drivingmissdaisy.co.nz

Conversation
Jooste, Hendrika (2020) *Pillars of Power*
www.pillarsofpower.com.au

FINAL BIG-PICTURE QUESTIONS

Books
Burns, Jim (2019) *Doing Life with Your Adult Children*, Zondervan: Grand Rapids, MI.

Pillemer, Karl (2020) *Fault Lines*, Avery/Random House: New York, NY.

Wassermann, Selma (2001) *The Long Distance Grandmother*, Hartley & Marks Publishers Inc: Vancouver, Canada.

Wilson, Sandra D. (2001) *Hurt People Hurt People*, Discovery House: Grand Rapids, MI.

Articles

Fivush, Robyn (2008) 'Remembering and reminiscing: How individual lives are constructed in family narratives', *Memory Studies,* Vol. 1, iss. 1, pp. 44-58.

Gemignani, Marco (2014) 'Memory, Remembering, and Oblivion in Active Narrative Interviewing', *Qualitative Inquiry,* Vol. 20, iss. 2, pp. 127-135.

Gosling, Peter (2007) cited in Parfitt, Jo 'Grandparenting from long-distance', *The Telegraph,*
https://www.telegraph.co.uk/expat/4204998/Grandparenting-from-long-distance.html

Granset.com (n.d.) 'Difficult daughter-in-law? How do you build a positive relationship with her?',
https://www.gransnet.com/relationships/daughter-in-law-relationship

Newman, Kira M. (2020, Jul 14) 'How Purpose Changes Across Your Lifetime', *Greater Good Magazine,*
https://greatergood.berkeley.edu/article/item/how_purpose_changes_across_your_lifetime

Niezink, Lidewij & Train, Katherine (2020, Sep 23) 'Preventing Conflict Through Self-Empathy', *Psychology Today,*
https://www.psychologytoday.com/nz/blog/empathic-intervision/202009/preventing-conflict-through-self-empathy?amp

Parks, Melissa (n.d.) 'The Difference Between Self-Compassion and Self-Pity', *Intentional Expat*, https://www.intentionalexpat.com/category/self-compassion/

Website
Sinek, Simon (n.d.) https://quotefancy.com/quote/1415744/Simon-Sinek-The-big-picture-doesn-t-just-come-from-distance-it-also-comes-from-time

Conversation
Terry, June (2019) LinkedIn https://www.linkedin.com/in/june-terry-45541b44/

A LAST WORD: VIRAL UNCERTAINTY

Books
Spoonley, Paul (2020) *The New New Zealand*, Massey University Press: Auckland, N.Z.

Articles
Bhondekar, Roshan (2017) 'Why Past is More Important Than 'Present'', *Medium.com*, https://medium.com/@roshan_b/why-past-is-more-important-than-present-f36054e30f08

Brumann, Christoph (1998) 'The Anthropological Study of Globalization. Towards an Agenda for the Second Phase', *Anthropos*, Vol. 93. pp. 495-506.

Hallett Mobbs, Carole (2020, May 6) 'Expat life vs Lockdown life', *ExpatChild.com* https://expatchild.com/expat-life-vs-lockdown-life/

Jaeger, Dr Sonia (2020, Jul 17) 'The Many Faces of Pandemic Grief',
https://sonia-jaeger.com/en/category/personal-thoughts/

Zappavigna, Adrianna (2020, Aug 23) 'Covid 19 coronavirus: Dr Anthony Fauci's virus message for Australians as global infections top 23 million', *NZ Herald,*
https://www.nzherald.co.nz/world/news/article.cfm?c_id=2&objectid=12358748

Email
MacRae, Graeme (2020, Jan 1) Email to ASAANZ (Association of Social Anthropologists of Aotearoa/New Zealand).

Quahe, Yvonne (2020)
https://www.linkedin.com/in/yvonne-quahe-6083ab32/

Websites
International Association for Medical Assistance to Travellers (IAMAT)
https://www.iamat.org/coronavirus-covid-19-q-a

IATA
https://www.iatatravelcentre.com/international-travel-document-news/1580226297.htm

About the Author

Helen Ellis is a New Zealand researcher, writer, anthropologist and a veteran of Distance Grandparenting. Three of her four children and five of her six grandchildren live 16 to 30 flight hours away in America, England and Scotland.

In her research she asked the question: "How is distance grandparenting for you?" As a Distance Grandparent of more than 20 years, she has well and truly got the T-shirt. Her book, *Being a Distance Grandparent - a Book for ALL Generations*, combines that experience with her extensive global research. Helen feels passionately that Distance Parents and Distance Grandparents deserve a voice and has single-handedly and doggedly taken on that role. Her goal is to support each generation to understand how it is for the other.

"With understanding comes empathy and this can only do good as we all gingerly navigate the oftentimes challenging social phenomenon of distance families," she explains.

This is the first of a three-book series about distance families - each publication focussing on a different generation (grandparents, sons and daughters and grandchildren). Helen encourages *all* generations to read *all* three books.

For an update on all titles you are invited to visit www.DistanceFamilies.com.

Acknowledgements

I wish to thank those who partnered alongside me as my ideas came to fruition and this book project evolved.

Thank you to fellow anthropology students and the staff at Massey University, who graciously accepted that my foray at university had finality and that I'd be out the door as soon as I pressed the submit button on my research thesis - and I was. I had a crazy book-writing plan and you've taken an interest, which I've appreciated.

As I launched myself into a new world of authorship, global mobility and social media well-wishers appeared from here and there and together transported me from the new gal in town to a welcomed and respected member of their tribe. A special thanks to all those at Families in Global Transition (FIGT).

Thank you to my fellow Summertime Publishing first-time authors Rhoda Bangerter, Keri Bloomfield and Yvonne Quahe. Sharing our 2020 lockdown, in-the-trenches, writing odysseys meant a lot. You have important messages to share and I wish you the greatest success.

Thank you also to those distance daughters who shared wisdom from their perspective, especially Dr Karen Eriksen, Hendrika Jooste, Sundae Schneider-Bean and Anna Seidel. You made a difference. To my first readers, thank you for your time and for your passion about the topic.

My husband, Clive, has supported my research and writing and patiently listened to my thoughts, concerns and ponderings. My mother, Colleen, has been the chairperson of my fan club, always cheering me along. A special thank you to my children, stepchildren and grandchildren who have never faltered in their support of my work, even when they found their lives in print. I have learnt from you all; your travels and lives have opened up a world to me I would never have known and I am grateful.

Summertime Publishing's Managing Editor, Jo Parfitt, took me on, sight unseen. Her standards are high and like me she is a planner, which I've appreciated. She never hesitated to say a spade is a spade and I respect that quality about her. My book is a better one because of Jo. Behind the scenes was a publishing team who've been a pleasure to work with. Jack, Joshua, Paddy and Cath quietly and professionally dressed my book in its Sunday best.

Finally, I thank all the grandparents who have contributed to this book. First, my university research participant friends who opened their hearts and homes to my questions. They did not mind that their lives would end up in print and genuinely wanted to give a voice to the phenomenon of Distance Grandparenting. From there, my Distance Grandparent friends expanded around the globe as we chatted via Zoom. Thank you for all your stories and trust.

I acknowledge the recent passing of two grandfathers from my original research, Jim (N.Z./England) and Barry (N.Z./Scotland). I am grateful for their from-the-heart reflections and when I attended both memorial gatherings and the subject of their roles as grandfathers were mentioned, I knew I had got their stories right.

Helen Ellis
Founder
www.DistanceFamilies.com
Auckland
New Zealand

Also in the *Being a Distance* Series:

For an update on these titles please visit
www.DistanceFamilies.com.

BEING A
Distance Grandchild

A BOOK FOR ALL GENERATIONS

HELEN ELLIS
JOSHUA PARFITT

Also by Summertime Publishing and Springtime Books

TERRY ANNE WILSON
& JO PARFITT

MONDAY MORNING EMAILS

Six months, twelve countries, a thousand thoughts — two mothers share the journey of living a global life

with Lesley Lewis, Jan Mandy, Becky Grappo, Ellen Mahoney, Colleen Reichrath-Smith, Ruth Van Reken, Annette Graham and Neil Smith

"AN OUTSTANDING NEW ADDITION
TO THE GLOBAL FAMILY LITERATURE"
ROBIN PASCOE

THIS MESSY MOBILE LIFE

HOW A MOLA CAN HELP GLOBALLY MOBILE FAMILIES CREATE A LIFE BY DESIGN

MARIAM NAVAID OTTIMOFIORE

Helena Jalanka

greetings from

ABROADLAND

EXPERIENCES OF FAMILY LIFE ABROAD

with 70 Survive & Thrive Tips and 35 Real-Life Cartoons

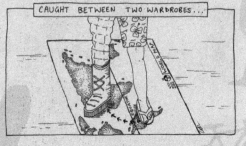

LIVING ELSEWHERE

Because a life overseas can be tough
and, well, sometimes you just have to laugh

CAUGHT BETWEEN TWO WARDROBES...

Cath Brew

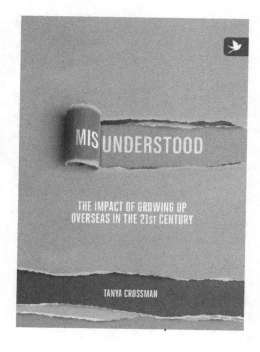

FOREWORD BY DOUG OTA

EMOTIONAL RESILIENCE
AND THE EXPAT CHILD

Practical tips and storytelling techniques
that will strengthen the global family

Julia Simens

CPSIA information can be obtained
at www.ICGtesting.com
Printed in the USA
BVHW040355140421
604820BV00005B/370